SEC. 498A OF I. P. C.- SUPREME COURT'S LEADING CASE LAWS

CASE NOTES- FACTS- FINDINGS OF APEX COURT JUDGES & CITATIONS

JAYPRAKASH BANSILAL SOMANI

Dedicated

To

All the Past & Present Judges of the Supreme Court of India.

Salute to their wisdom.

Salute to their interpretation of Law.

Salute to their elaborative judgement writing.

Enter Caption

Contents

Preface

Dear Learned Advocates of the Trial Courts, Family Court, Session Courts, Tribunals, High Courts, Supreme Court & Individuals,

I am very delighted to provide you a book on 'SEC. 498A OF I. P. C.- Supreme Court of India's Leading Case Laws'.

In this book you will get...

1. Name of the Case i. e. Cause title

2.Relevant Sections discussed in the case

3. Hon'ble Judges/Coram of the case

4.Number of PDF Pages in Original Judgement of the case

5. All available Citations of the case

6. Case Note with appeal allowed/ dismissed or disposed off

7. Facts of the case

8. Hon'ble Apex Court's findings, while dismissing/allowing or disposing the appeal

9. Ratio Decidendi if any.

My special thanks to Manupatra, because of their web portal I can compile this book in well manner. I am also thankful to Notion Press to support me to publish & market this book throughout the Country. Thanks to my Juniors, Advocate Colleagues & Insolvency Professional Colleagues to support me in this venture.

Adv. Aqsa Sahar has helped me a lot to compile this book.

I hope this book will add some value addition in the wealth of your legal knowledge. Your positive feedbacks will boost me to compile/ write further books & negative feedbacks will improve my skills. Kindly send your valuable feedbacks by email.

Thanks with Regards,

Jayprakash B. Somani

Advocate, Supreme Court of India

Email: jaysomani64@gmail.com

Web Site:www.jayprakashsomani.com

Call: 9318381287, 8384051134, 9322188701.

Acknowledgements

Printed & Published by
Notion Press
No. 8, 3rd Cross Street,
CIT Colony, Mylapore,
Chennai, Tamil Nadu- 600004

ᐅᐅᐅ

Managed by
Jayprakash Somani Advocates & Solicitors
Law Firm for Supreme Court of India
Delhi Office
257 C, Pocket 1, Mayur Vihar Phase 1, Delhi 110091.
Call 9318381287, 8384051134, 9322188701, 8459194576.
Supreme Court Chamber
312, 3rd Floor, M. C. Setalvad Block, In front of 'D' Gate, Bhagwan Das Road, Supreme Court of India, New Delhi 110001
Contact: 8459194576, 9811011747,
www.jayprakashsomani.com

ᐅᐅᐅ

Books are available online at
1. Notion Press: https://notionpress.com/author/jayprakash_somani
2. Amazon: https://www.amazon.in/s?k=jayprakash+somani
3. Flipkart: https://www.flipkart.com/search?q=Jayprakash%20Somani

ᐅᐅᐅ

ONE

KASHMIRA DEVI VS. STATE OF UTTARAKHAND AND ORS., 2020

Hon'ble Judges/Coram:

R. Banumathi and A.S. Bopanna, JJ.

Relevant Sections:

SECTIONS 498-A AND 304-B OF IPC, SECTION 113-B OF EVIDENCE ACT.

No. of pdf Pages of the Original Judgment: 10

Equivalent Citation:

2020(211)AIC226, AIR2020SC652, 2020 (1) ALD(Crl.) 334 (SC), 2020 (112) ACC 841, 2021 (1) ALT (Crl.) 462 (A.P.), 2020(2)BLJ33, (2020)3CALLT75(SC), 129(2020)CLT452, 2020CriLJ1343, 2020(1)Crimes144(SC), 2020(4)Crimes93(SC), I(2020)DMC414SC, 2020(2)JKJ264[SC], 2020(1)RCR(Criminal)892, (2020)11SCC343, 2020 (3) SCJ 268, 2020(1)UC662 MANU/SC/0091/2020

Case Notes:

Criminal - Conviction - Legality - Sections 304-B and 498-A of Indian Penal Code, 1860 (IPC) - Instant appeal had been filed by Appellant assailing impugned judgment passed by High Court whereby High Court had allowed appeal filed by Respondent and set aside acquittal of Appellant passed by trial court and convicted Appellant for charges under Sections 304-B and 498-A of IPC - Whether impugned order of conviction was liable to be set aside.

Facts:

The case of the prosecution in brief is that the marriage between deceased/Urmila @ Guddi and Proforma Respondent No. 3/Jagdish Singh was solemnized four years back. At the time of the marriage dowry was given by parents of the deceased as per their financial capacity; despite the same the husband and in-laws of the deceased were not satisfied. The trial court acquitted Appellant and the other Accused persons for the charges Under Section 304-B and 498-A of IPC stating that the prosecution has failed to prove the case against the Accused persons beyond reasonable doubt. Being aggrieved by the order, an appeal was filed by the State of Uttarakhand, whereby High Court set aside the order passed by the Trial Court and convicted Appellant under Section 304-B read with Section 498-A of the IPC. There is close proximity between demand of dowry for which deceased was harassed and tortured by her in-laws and her death. With these findings, the High Court allowed the appeal filed by the Respondent and set aside the order of acquittal passed by the trial court and convicted them. Held, while allowing the appeal in part 1. In the present case, from the evidence of PW-1, prosecution has proved that soon before the death", deceased was subjected to cruelty and harassment. When prosecution has established that deceased was subjected to dowry harassment "soon before the death" and that within seven years of marriage deceased Urmila had died an unnatural death, the presumption Under Section 113-B of the Evidence Act is to be raised against the Appellant that she caused the dowry death. Once the prosecution is able to establish the ingredients of Section 304B Indian Penal Code, it is for the Accused to rebut the presumption. But the Accused have not adduced any reliable evidence to rebut the presumption. The evidence of DW-1 and DW-2 relating to the incident will not be sufficient when the incident is viewed keeping in perspective the evidence of prosecution relating to the demand for dowry preceding the actual incident. In fact, when the deceased was shifted from Kota hospital, Srinagar to Dehradun hospital, PW-1 tried to accompany them but the Accused refused to take PW-1 along. Not informing about the incident and refusal of the Appellant and other Accused to take PW-1 along with them to the hospital, are strong circumstances against the Appellant. While arriving at such conclusion the High Court has kept in view a decision of this Court in the case of Nallam Veera Stayanandam and Ors. v. The Public Prosecutor, High Court of A.P. wherein it is held that each dying declaration has to be considered independently on its own merit as to its evidentiary value and one cannot be rejected because of the contents of the other. It is held therein that the Court has to consider each of them in its correct perspective and satisfy itself which one of them reflects the true state of affairs. The consideration made herein above would also indicate that on an independent consideration, the dying declaration dated 13.02.2008 is reliable for the reasons stated above. To the same effect the High Court has also relied on another decision of this Court in the case of Ashabai and Anr. v. State of Maharashtra wherein it is held that when there are multiple dying declarations, each dying declaration has to be separately assessed and evaluated on its own merits. The High Court has also taken note of a decision of this Court in the case of State of Karnataka v. Suvarnamma and Anr. wherein it is held that the dying declaration recorded by the police officer was consistent with the circumstances on record while dying declaration recorded by the Magistrate was not found to be consistent. The validity of the statement so recorded, therefore, stands established. Hence the High Court having examined the matter threadbare has arrived at its conclusion in recording the conviction in the manner as it has done which is justified and does not call for interference. The High Court has awarded life imprisonment to the Appellant on being convicted Under Section 304B Indian Penal Code. The minimum sentence provided is seven years but it may extend to imprisonment for life. In fact, this Court in the case of Hem Chand v. State of Haryana has held that while imposing the sentence, awarding extreme punishment of imprisonment for life Under Section 304B of IPC should be in rare cases and not in every case. Though the mitigating factor noticed in the said case was different, in the instant case keeping in view the age of the Appellant and also the contribution that would be required by her to the family, while husband is also aged and further taking into consideration all other circumstances, the sentence as awarded by the High Court to the Appellant herein is liable to be modified. The conviction of the Appellant recorded by the High Court under Section 304-B of IPC and Section 498-A of IPC through its judgment is upheld and affirmed. The sentence ordered by the High Court through its order is modified and the sentence of imprisonment for life is altered by ordering the Appellant to undergo rigorous imprisonment for a period of seven years which shall include the period of sentence already undergone by the Appellant. The fine as imposed and the default sentence is sustained. The appeal is allowed in part.

Hon'ble Apex Court Held, while dismissing/ allowing the appeal:

In appeal before us, Appellant has contended that the High Court erred in ignoring that the prosecution failed to present any material to Rule out the possibility of an accidental death so as to bring it within the purview of the 'Death occurring otherwise than in normal circumstances' as required Under Section 304-B of Indian Penal Code and further failed in establishing the fact that soon before the occurrence there was cruelty/harassment in relation to dowry demand and to bring on record any reliable evidence of a subsisting dowry demand. Further the High Court erred in ignoring the fact that the parents of the deceased never made an attempt to report that there was a demand for dowry to the police or the elders of the locality and the fact that the allegation regarding dowry was made for the first time on 15.02.2008 while the incident took place on 06.02.2008. It is also contended by the Appellant that High Court erred in convicting the Accused by reversing the judgment of acquittal of the Appellant even though the same was based on reasonable and plausible grounds and in ignoring the evidences brought on record and the credibility of the prosecution witnesses. It is also submitted by the Appellant that the High Court erred by relying on the three-dying declarations of the deceased in isolation and failed to consider the possibility that the third dying declaration of the deceased was a result of being brainwashed by her parents. It is the contention of the Appellant that error was committed by the Court in bringing the case within the ambit of the Section 113-B of the Indian Evidence Act by proceeding under the presumption arising Under Section 304-A and 113-B of the Indian Evidence Act.

ORDER

(i) The conviction of the Appellant recorded by the High Court Under Section 304-B Indian Penal Code and Section 498-A Indian Penal Code through its judgment dated 29.06.2017 is upheld and affirmed.

(ii) The sentence ordered by the High Court through its order dated 10.07.2017 is modified and the sentence of imprisonment for life is altered by ordering the Appellant to undergo rigorous imprisonment for a period of seven years which shall include the period of sentence already undergone by the Appellant. The fine as imposed and the default sentence is sustained.

(iii) The appeal is allowed in part, in the above terms.

(iv) The parties to bear their own cost.

Pending application, if any, shall stand disposed of.

TWO

GEETA MEHROTRA AND ORS. VS. STATE OF U.P. AND ORS., 2012

Hon'ble Judges/Coram:

T.S. Thakur and Gyan Sudha Misra, JJ.

Relevant Sections:

CRIMINAL MATTERS - MATTERS FOR/AGAINST QUASHING OF CRIMINAL PROCEEDINGS

No. of pdf Pages of the Original Judgment: 9

Equivalent Citation:

2013(2)ACR1963, 2012(10)ADJ464, 2012(120)AIC75, AIR2013SC181, AIR2013SC181, 2013(1) ALJ 126, 2013 (80) ACC 185, 2013(2)ALT(Cri)21, 2012(4)BLJ224, IV(2012)CCR405(SC), 2012 (3) CG.L.R.W. 242, 2012(2)HLR572, 2013(1)J.L.J.R.115, JT2012(11)SC46, 2013(I)OLR372, 2013(1)PLJR10, 2012(4)RCR(Criminal)812, 2013(2)RLW1087(SC), 2012(10)SCALE299, (2012)10SCC741, [2012]9SCR641, 2013(1)UC299 MANU/SC/0895/2012

Case Notes:

1. Criminal Procedure Code, 1973 - Sec. 482 - Cognizance under Secs. 498-A/323/504/506, IPC read with Sec. 3/4 of D.P. Act - Quashing of - Appeal before Apex Court against order of High Court - As per contents of FIR, there is no allegations against 'GM' and 'RM' except casual reference of their names who have been included in the FIR but mere casual reference of the names of the family members in a matrimonial dispute without allegation of active involvement in the matter would not justify taking cognizance against them overlooking the fact borne out of experience that there is

a tendency to involve the entire family members of the household in the domestic quarrel taking place in a matrimonial dispute specially if it happens soon after the wedding - Proceedings initiated against the appellants 'GM' and 'RM' quashed. Courts are expected to adopt a cautious approach in matters of quashing specially in cases of matrimonial dispute whether the FIR in fact discloses commission of an offence by the relatives of the principal accused or the FIR prima facie discloses a case of over-implication by involving the entire family of the accused at the instance of the complainant, who is out to settle her scores arising out of the teething problem or skirmish of domestic bickering while settling down in her new matrimonial surrounding.2. F.I.R. - If the FIR did not disclose the commission of an offence, the Court would be justified in quashing the proceedings preventing the abuse of the process of law.3. F.I.R. - If the FIR as it stands does not disclose specific allegation against accused more so against the co-accused specially in a matter arising out of matrimonial bickering, it would be clear abuse of the legal and judicial process to mechanically send the named accused in the FIR to undergo the trial unless of course the FIR discloses specific allegations which would persuade the Court to take cognizance of the offence alleged against the relatives of the main accused who are prima facie not found to have indulged in physical and mental torture of the complainant wife.

Facts:

This appeal by special leave in which we granted leave has been filed by the Appellants against the order dated 6.9.2010 passed by the High Court of Judicature at Allahabad in Crl. Miscellaneous Application No. 22714/2007 whereby the High Court had been pleased to dispose of the application moved by the Appellants under Section 482 Code of Criminal Procedure for quashing the order of the Magistrate taking cognizance against the Appellants under Sections 498A/323/504/506 Indian Penal Code read with Section 3/4 of the Dowry Prohibition Act with an observation that the question of territorial jurisdiction cannot be properly decided by the High Court under Section 482 Code of Criminal Procedure for want of adequate facts. It was, therefore, left open to the Appellants to move the trial court for dropping the proceedings on the ground of lack of territorial jurisdiction. The High Court however granted interim protection to the Appellants by directing the authorities not to issue coercive process against the Appellants until disposal of the application filed by the Appellants with a further direction to the trial court to dispose of the application if moved by the

Appellants, within a period of two months from the date of moving the application. The application under Section 482 Code of Criminal Procedure was thus disposed of by the High Court.

Hon'ble Apex Court Held, while dismissing/ allowing the appeal:

The High Court in our considered opinion appear to have missed that assuming the trial court had territorial jurisdiction, it was still left to be decided whether it was a fit case to send the Appellants for trial when the FIR failed to make out a prima facie case against them regarding the allegation of inflicting physical and mental torture to the complainant demanding dowry from the complainant. Since the High Court has failed to consider all these aspects, this Court as already stated hereinbefore, could have remitted the matter to the High Court to consider whether a case was made out against the Appellants to proceed against them. But as the contents of the FIR does not disclose specific allegation against the brother and sister of the complainant's husband except casual reference of their names, it would not be just to direct them to go through protracted procedure by remanding for consideration of the matter all over again by the High Court and make the unmarried sister of the main accused and his elder brother to suffer the ordeal of a criminal case pending against them specially when the FIR does not disclose ingredients of offence under Sections 498A/323/504/506, Indian Penal Code and Sections 3/4 of the Dowry Prohibition Act.

We, therefore, deem it just and legally appropriate to quash the proceedings initiated against the Appellants Geeta Mehrotra and Ramji Mehrotra as the FIR does not disclose any material which could be held to be constituting any offence against these two Appellants. Merely by making a general allegation that they were also involved in physical and mental torture of the complainant-Respondent No. 2 without mentioning even a single incident against them as also the fact as to how they could be motivated to demand dowry when they are only related as brother and sister of the complainant's husband, we are pleased to quash and set aside the criminal proceedings in so far as these Appellants are concerned and consequently the order passed by the High Court shall stand overruled. The appeal accordingly is allowed.

THREE

NAZMA VS. JAVED, 2012

Hon'ble Judges/Coram:

K.S. Panicker Radhakrishnan and Dipak Misra, JJ.

Relevant Sections:

CRIMINAL MATTERS - MATTERS RELATING TO HARASSMENT, CRUELTY TO WOMAN FOR DOWRY, DOWRY DEATH, EVE-TEASING, DOMESTIC VIOLENCE ETC.

No. of pdf Pages of the Original Judgment: 5

Equivalent Citation:

2012(120)AIC28, 2013 (80) ACC 182, 2013(3)ALT(Cri)189, 2012BomCR(Cri)841, IV(2012)CCR444(SC), 2013(1)CGLJ131, 2012(6)CTC587, 2013(1)HLR40, ILR2012(4)Kerala365, 2012(4)J.L.J.R.360, 2012MLJ(Crl)573, 2013(I)OLR532, 2013(I)OLR(SC)532, 2012(4)PLJR257, 2013(1)RCR(Criminal)83, 2012(10)SCALE494, (2013)1SCC376, [2012]9SCR826, 2013(1)UC213 MANU/SC/0906/2012

Case Notes:

Criminal Procedure Code, 1973 - Secs. 439, 482 - Constitution of India - Arts. 226 and 227 - Criminal miscellaneous application in a disposed of writ petition - Order not to arrest - Jurisdiction vested on the High Court under Articles 226 and 227 of the Constitution of India as well as Section 482 of Cr.P.C. are all exceptional in nature and to be used in most exceptional cases - Jurisdiction under Sec. 439, Cr.P.C. is also discretionary and it is required to be exercised with great care and caution - Grant of bail or not to grant, is within the powers of the regular criminal Court and the High Court, in its inherent jurisdiction, not justified in usurping their powers - Once the criminal writ petition has been disposed of, the High Court becomes functus officio and cannot entertain review petitions or miscellaneous applications except for carrying out typographical or clerical errors - In the present case, High Court has entertained a petition in a disposed of criminal writ petition and granted reliefs, which is impermissible in law.

Facts:

The marriage of the Appellant and 1st Respondent took place in the year 1997 according to the Muslim rites and customs and out of that wedlock three children were born. According to the Appellant, 1st Respondent married again for a third time. During the subsistence of the Appellant's marriage, 1st Respondent kept on harassing the Appellant demanding dowry, which resulted in the lodgment of an F.I.R. by the Appellant's brother, being F.I.R. No. 72 of 2003, on 5.8.2003 and a case was registered under Sections 498-A, 323, 324, 504, 506 of the Indian Penal Code (Indian Penal Code) and Sections 3 and 4 of the Dowry Prohibition Act against 1st Respondent and his family members. The case was later transferred to the Ladies Police Station, Rakab Ganj, Agra vide an order dated 12.9.2003 of the S.S.P., Agra.

Family members of 1st Respondent then approached the High Court of Allahabad and filed a Criminal Miscellaneous Writ Petition No. 5426 of 2003 for quashing the F.I.R. In that writ petition, the Appellant was not made a party, but only her brother. The family members of 1st Respondent had submitted before the High Court that an amount of Rs. 2,000/- per month would be deposited in the Court of the Chief Judicial Magistrate, until the conclusion of the trial and the Appellant could withdraw the same.

Hon'ble Apex Court Held, while dismissing/ allowing the appeal:

Leave granted.

We are of the view that the High Court has committed a grave error in not only entertaining the criminal miscellaneous application in a disposed of writ petition, but also passing an order not to arrest the 1st Respondent till the conclusion of the trial. Grant of bail or not to grant, is within the powers of the regular Criminal Court and the High Court, in its inherent jurisdiction, not justified in usurping their powers. Once the criminal writ petition has been disposed of, the High Court becomes *functus officio* and cannot entertain review petitions or miscellaneous applications except for carrying out typographical or clerical errors. In the instant case, the High Court has entertained a petition in a disposed of criminal writ petition and granted reliefs, which is impermissible in law.

We are, therefore, inclined to allow this appeal and set aside the impugned order passed by the High Court, with costs of Rs. 25,000/- to be paid by 1st Respondent to the Appellant, within a period of two months.

FOUR

M. Radha Hari Seshu Vs. The State of Telangana, 2020

Hon'ble Judges/Coram:

Ashok Bhushan and R. Subhash Reddy, JJ.

Relevant Sections:

CRIMINAL MATTERS - CRIMINAL MATTERS RELATING TO SUSPENSION OF SENTENCE

No. of pdf Pages of the Original Judgment: 4

Equivalent Citation:

2020(213)AIC1, AIR2020SC4154, 2020 (113) ACC 359, 2020(5)BLJ369, 2020(3)Crimes192(SC), (2020)8SCC114, 2020 (7-8) SCJ 342, 2020(2)UC1275 MANU/SC/0590/2020

Case Note:

Criminal - Suspension of sentence - Sections 302, 304B and 498A of Indian Penal Code, 1860 - Case was registered against Appellant and his parents for alleged offences under Sections 498A, 304B and 302 of Code - After completion of investigation, chargesheet was filed against the Appellant-Accused No. 1, and his parents - Accused Nos. 2 and 3 for offence under Sections 304B and 498A of Code - Court of Sessions had convicted Appellant for offence under Sections 304B and 498A of Code - Accused Nos. 2 and 3 in said case were discharged - Appellant had preferred appeal before High Court seeking suspension of sentence and to release Appellant on bail, pending disposal of criminal appeal - Such application filed by Appellant was dismissed by High Court - Hence, present appeal - Whether it was fit case to suspend sentence imposed on Appellant pending Criminal Appeal before High Court.

Facts:

Based on the complaint filed by the de facto complainant a case was registered against the Appellant and his parents for the alleged offences under Sections 498A, 304B and 302, Indian Penal Code (IPC). After completion of investigation, chargesheet was filed against the Appellant-Accused No. 1, and his parents - Accused Nos. 2 and 3 for the offence under Sections 304B and 498A, Indian Penal Code. The Metropolitan Magistrate took cognizance of the case against the Accused for the offences under Sections 304B and 498A, Indian Penal Code and committed it to the Court of Sessions. The Additional District and Sessions Judge had convicted the Appellant for offence under Sections 304B and 498A of Indian Penal Code. Accused Nos. 2 and 3 in the said case were discharged on an application filed by them, as such, Appellant alone was tried for the offence under Sections 498A and 304B Indian Penal Code. The Appellant had preferred appeal before the High Court seeking suspension of sentence and to release the Appellant on bail, pending disposal of the criminal appeal. Such application filed by the Appellant was dismissed by the High Court.

Hon'ble Apex Court Held, while dismissing/ allowing the appeal:

Held, while allowing the appeal:

(i) It was to be noted that marriage of the deceased with Appellant was performed and they were blessed with two children. Though initially case was registered under Sections 304B, 498A and 302, Indian Penal Code, after investigation the Appellant and his parents were charged under Sections 304B and 498A, Indian Penal Code. The parents of the Appellant were discharged on an application and only Appellant was tried for the offence under Sections 498A and 304B, Indian Penal Code. It was also brought to our notice that the Appellant was confined in jail and further it was also brought to our notice that the father of the Appellant was diagnosed with pancolitis.

(ii) Though Counsel of Appellant, by taking this court to the findings recorded by the trial court, had submitted that no case was made out for the offence under Section 304B and he was erroneously convicted for offence under Section 304B as well as 498A, Indian Penal Code, in view of the pendency of the appeal before the High Court, this court did not wish to go into the merits of the matter at this stage. Therefore, deem it appropriate that it was a fit case to suspend the sentence imposed on the Appellant and to enlarge the Appellant on bail, pending Criminal Appeal before the High Court.

ppp

FIVE

VIPIN JAISWAL (A-I) VS. STATE OF A.P. REP. BY PUB. PROSECUTOR, 2013

Hon'ble Judges/Coram:

A.K. Patnaik and S.J. Mukhopadhaya, JJ

Relevant Sections:

CRIMINAL MATTERS - MATTERS RELATING TO HARASSMENT, CRUELTY TO WOMAN FOR DOWRY, DOWRY DEATH, EVE-TEASING, DOMESTIC VIOLENCE ETC.

No. of pdf Pages of the Original Judgment: 6

Equivalent Citation:

2013iv AD (S.C.) 275, 2013(125)AIC194, AIR2013SC1567, 2013(2) AKR 339, 2013(1)ALD(Cri)967, 2013 (82) ACC 61, 2013(2)ALT(Cri)457, 2013(2)BLJ130, 2013(3)B.L.J.531, II(2013)CCR45(SC), 116(2013)CLT563, 2013CriLJ2095, 2013(3)Crimes229(SC), 1(2013)DMC700, (2013)3GLR2510, 2013(1)HLR598, 2013(2)J.L.J.R.440, 2013(2)JCC1330, JT2013(4)SC188, 2013(II)OLR130, 2013(3)PLJR91, 2013(2)RCR(Criminal)342, 2013(3)SCALE525, (2013)3SCC684, [2013]3SCR449 MANU/SC/0253/2013

Case Notes:

Penal Code, 1860 - Secs. 304B and 498A - Conviction under - On appeal High Court acquitted the two other relatives of the appellant but maintained the conviction of the appellant-Appeal - In any case to hold an accused guilty of both the offences under Secs. 304B and 498A, the prosecution is required to prove beyond reasonable doubt that the deceased was subjected to cruelty or harassment by the accused - Evidence of the prosecution witnesses, and in particular P.W. 1 and P.W. 4 shows that they have made general allegations of harassment by the appellant towards the deceased and have not brought in evidence any specific acts of cruelty or harassment by the appellant on the deceased - Held, since the prosecution has not been able to prove beyond reasonable doubt this ingredient of harassment or cruelty, neither of the offences under Sec. 498-A and 304-B IPC has been made out by the prosecution. In our considered opinion, the evidence of DW 1 (the appellant) and Ext. D19 cast a reasonable doubt on the prosecution story that the deceased was subjected to harassment or cruelty in connection with demand of dowry. In our view, onus was on the prosecution to prove beyond reasonable doubt the ingredient of Section 498A, IPC and the essential ingredient of offence under Section 498A is that the accused, as the husband of the deceased, has subjected her to cruelty as defined in the Explanation to Section 498A, IPC. Similarly, for the Court to draw the presumption under Section 113B of the Evidence Act that the appellant had caused dowry death as defined in Section 304B, IPC, the prosecution has to prove besides the demand of dowry, harassment or cruelty caused by the accused to the deceased soon before her death.

Facts:

The facts briefly are that an FIR was lodged by Gynaneshwar Jaiswal on 4.4.1999 at 2.15 p.m. in Mangalhat Police Station, Hyderabad. In the FIR it was stated by the informant that his daughter Meenakshi Jaiswal was married to the Appellant on 22.2.1996 and at the time of marriage he gave sufficient gold jewellery, silver items, furniture, electrophonic gadgets etc., worth above Rs. 2,50,000/- but ever since her marriage, she was subjected to physical and mental torture by her husband Vipin Jaiswal, her husband's parents Prem Kumar Jaiswal and Yashoda Bai and her husband's sister Supriya and her husband and they all brutally assaulted her on innumerable occasions for not getting sufficient dowry. It was further stated in the FIR that on 2.4.1999 the informant received a call from the Appellant and he went to the house of the Appellant along with his relatives to find out what had happened as well as to give invitation for a function at his place but they all abused him and the Appellant physically assaulted and pushed him out from the house but fearing the safety of his daughter and her welfare, he did not report the matter to the police. It is further stated in the FIR that on 4.4.1999 at about 1.00 p.m. when he came back home, he was informed on telephone by his son that Meenakshi had received severe burn injuries and as a result died in the house of the Appellant. The police registered a Criminal Case under Section 304B, Indian Penal Code and took up investigation and submitted a charge-sheet against the Appellant and his other relatives under Sections 304B and 498A, Indian Penal Code.

Ratio Decidendi:

"Conviction of the accused shall be made only when there are evidences proving his guilt beyond reasonable doubt."

Hon'ble Apex Court Held, while dismissing/ allowing the appeal:

In our considered opinion, the evidence of DW1 (the Appellant) and Ext. D19 cast a reasonable doubt on the prosecution story that the deceased was subjected to harassment or cruelty in connection with demand of dowry. In our view, onus was on the prosecution to prove beyond reasonable doubt the ingredient of Section 498A, Indian Penal Code and the essential ingredient of offence under Section 498A is that the accused, as the husband of the deceased, has subjected her to cruelty as defined in the Explanation to Section 498A, Indian Penal Code. Similarly, for the Court to draw the presumption under Section 113B of the Evidence Act that the Appellant had caused dowry death as defined in Section 304B, Indian Penal Code, the prosecution has to prove besides the demand of dowry, harassment or cruelty caused by the accused to the deceased soon before her death. Since the prosecution has not been able to prove beyond reasonable doubt this ingredient of harassment or cruelty, neither of the offences under Sections 498A and 304B, Indian Penal Code has been made out by the prosecution.

We accordingly allow this appeal, set aside the impugned judgment of the High Court and that of the Trial Court and direct that the bail bond furnished by the Appellant shall stand discharged.

SIX

Lalit Kumar Jain Vs. Union of India and Ors., 2021

Hon'ble Judges/Coram:

Dipak Misra, Ashok Bhushan and R. Banumathi, JJ. L. Nageswara Rao and S. Ravindra Bhat, JJ.

Relevant Sections:

COMPANY LAW, MRTP AND ALLIED MATTERS

No. of pdf Pages of the Original Judgment: 47

Equivalent Citation:

IV(2021)BC393(SC), 2021 (2) CCC 273 , (2021)4CompLJ305(SC), 2022(1)RCR(Civil)41, (2021)9SCC321, 2021 (4) SCJ 542, [2021]167SCL1(SC) MANU/SC/0352/2021

Case Notes:

Constitution - Vires and validity of Notification dated 15.11.2019 (Impugned Notification) - Article 32 of the Constitution of India, 1950 - Notification stated to be issued in excess of the authority conferred upon the Union of India - Impugned notification brought into force Section 2(e), Section 78 (except with regard to fresh start process), Sections 79, 94-187 (both inclusive); Section 239(2)(g), (h) & (i); Section 239(2)(m) to (zc); Section 239(2)(zn) to (zs) and Section 249 of the Insolvency and Bankruptcy Code, 2016 (IBC).

Facts:

The principal ground of attack in the set of instant petitions was that the executive government could not have selectively brought into force the

IBC and applied some of its provisions to one sub-category of individuals, i.e., personal guarantors to corporate creditors. All the Petitioners argued that the impugned notification, in seeking to achieve that end, is ultra vires. This argument is premised on the nature and content of Section 1(3), which the Petitioners characterize to be conditional legislation. Unlike delegated legislation, they say, conditional legislation is a limited power which can be exercised once, in respect of the subject matter or class of subject matters. As long as different dates are designated for bringing into force the enactment, or in relation to different areas, the executive acts within its powers. However, when it selectively does so, and segregates the subject matter of coverage of the enactment, it indulges in impermissible legislation.

Hon'ble Apex Court Held, while dismissing/ allowing the appeal:

Held, while dismissing the Petition:

The impugned notification operationalizes the Code so far as it relates to personal guarantors to corporate debtors: (1) Section 79 pertains to the definitional Section for the purposes of insolvency resolution and bankruptcy for individuals before the Adjudicating Authority. (2) Section 94 to 187 outline the entire structure regarding initiation of the resolution process for individuals before the Adjudicating Authority.

The impugned notification authorises the Central Government and the Board to frame Rules and Regulations on how to allow the pending actions against a personal guarantor to a corporate debtor before the Adjudicating Authority. The intent of the notification, facially, is to allow for pending proceedings to be adjudicated in terms of the Code.

Parliamentary intent was to treat personal guarantors differently from other categories of individuals.

Impugned notification not an instance of legislative exercise, or amounting to impermissible and selective application of provisions of the Code. There is no compulsion in the Code that it should, at the same time, be made applicable to all individuals, (including personal guarantors) or not at all. There is sufficient indication in the Code-by Section 2(e), Section 5(22), Section 60 and Section 179 indicating that personal guarantors, though forming part of the larger grouping of individuals, were to be, in view of their intrinsic connection with corporate debtors, dealt with differently, through the same adjudicatory process and by the same forum (though not insolvency provisions) as such corporate debtors.

Approval of a resolution plan does not ipso facto discharge a personal guarantor (of a corporate debtor) of her or his liabilities under the contract of guarantee. As held by this Court, the release or discharge of a principal borrower from the debt owed by it to its creditor, by an involuntary process, i.e. by operation of law, or due to liquidation or insolvency proceeding, does not absolve the surety/guarantor of his or her liability, which arises out of an independent contract.

Impugned notification legal and valid. The writ petitions, transferred cases and transfer petitions are accordingly dismissed in the above terms, without order on costs.

SEVEN

GUMANSINH AND ORS. VS. THE STATE OF GUJARAT, 2021

Honb'le Judges/Coram:

S. Abdul Nazeer and Krishna Murari, JJ

Relevant Sections:

CRIMINAL MATTERS - MATTERS RELATING TO HARASSMENT, CRUELTY TO WOMAN FOR DOWRY, DOWRY DEATH, EVE-TEASING, DOMESTIC VIOLENCE ETC.

No. of pdf Pages of the Original Judgments: 13

Equivalent Citation:

2021(226)AIC261, AIR2021SC4174, 2022 (1) ALT (Crl.) 7 (A.P.), 2021(6)BLJ16, 2021CriLJ4507, 2021(3)Crimes326(SC), III(2021)DMC338SC, 2021(3)HLR611, 2021(4)JKJ157[SC], 2021(4)RCR(Criminal)111 MANU/SC/0596/2021

Case Notes:

Criminal - Conviction - Sections 306 and 498A read with Section 114 of the Indian Penal Code, 1860 (IPC) - Trial Court held prosecution to have successfully established charges framed against Appellants - High Court in appeal confirmed findings arrived at by Trial Court - Hence, the present appeal - Whether prosecution established charge of abatement and dowry demand against the Appellants?

Facts:

Appellant No. 1 was married to Deceased. As alleged, A1 always used to ask deceased to money bring her father (PW1). Due to poor financial condition, PW-1 was not able to satisfy the demand of A1. This caused deceased to suffer beatings at the hands of A1 and A2, her mother-n-law also used to pick up quarrel with deceased on one pretext or the other. The deceased eventually committed suicide by consuming poison at her matrimonial home. Trial Court convicted the Appellants. High Court in appeal observed that the evidence produced by the prosecution clearly indicated that deceased was subjected to mental and physical cruelty by the Appellants and thus confirmed the conviction. Hence, the present appeal.

Hon'ble Apex Court Held, while dismissing/ allowing the appeal:
Held, while dismissing the Appeals:

In the case at hands, PW-1, 2, 3 and 4, though they are related to the deceased, are natural witnesses. There being no bar in examining the family members or any other person as witnesses, their evidence is not liable to be discarded on this ground.

The prosecution has been successful in proving the charge of cruelty under Explanation (b) of Section 498-A Indian Penal Code.

There is no dispute about the facts that the deceased committed suicide within a period of seven years from the date of her marriage and charged-Accused had subjected her to cruelty.

Admittedly, in the case at hands, the evidence clearly establishes the offence of cruelty or harassment caused to the deceased and thus the foundation for the presumption exists. Admittedly the Appellants have led no evidence to rebut the presumption.

Courts below committed no illegality in holding that the Accused-Appellants abetted the suicide of the deceased.

Both the Trial Court as well as the High Court have threadbare considered the evidence and have recorded cogent reasons to come to the conclusion that the prosecution has been successful in proving the case against the Appellants beyond reasonable doubt.

No reason to interfere with the impugned judgment. The appeals are, therefore, dismissed.

EIGHT

Naresh Kumar Mangla Vs. Anita Agarwal and Ors., 2020

Hon'ble Judges/Coram:

Dr. D.Y. Chandrachud, Indu Malhotra and Indira Banerjee, JJ.

Relevant Sections:

CRIMINAL MATTERS - CRIMINAL MATTERS RELATING TO CANCELLATION TO BAIL

No. of pdf Pages of the Original Judgment: 16

Equivalent Citation:

2020(12)ADJ622, AIR2021SC277, 2021ALLMR(Cri)3084, 2021CriLJ2066, 2021(1)Crimes105(SC), I(2021)DMC62SC, 2021(1)HLR271, 2021(1)JKJ293[SC], 2021(1)MLJ(Crl)170, 2021 (1) MWN (CR.) 109, 2021(1)N.C.C.128, 2020(Suppl.)Sim.L.C. 401, 2021(1)UC231 MANU/SC/0951/2020

Case Note:

Criminal - Anticipatory bail - Cancellation of - Sections 304-B, 313, 323, 498-A and 506 of Indian Penal Code, 1860 and Sections 3 and 4 of Dowry Prohibition Act, 1961 - Applications for anticipatory bail filed by four out of five persons who had been named as Accused in case registered under Sections 498A, 304-B, 323, 506 and 313 of Code and Sections 3/4 of Act - Husband of deceased was in custody - Single Judge of High Court allowed applications and granted them anticipatory bail - Hence, present appeal -

Whether High Court erred in granting anticipatory bail to accused persons.

Facts:

FIR was registered against accused persons for offence under Sections 498A, 304-B, 323, 506 and 313 of the Indian Penal Code and Sections 3/4 of the Dowry Prohibition Act, 1961. The Sessions Judge noted that besides naming the Accused specifically, there were also allegations against the four Respondents in the FIR of torturing the deceased and of making demands for dowry. Non-bailable warrants were issued against the four Accused. Applications for anticipatory bail were filed on their behalf before the High Court. A Single Judge of the High Court allowed the applications and granted them anticipatory bail.

Hon'ble Apex Court Held, while dismissing/ allowing the appeal:

Held, while allowing the appeal:

(i) The judgment of the Single Judge of the High Court was unsustainable. The FIR contains a recital of allegations bearing on the role of the Accused in demanding dowry, of the prior incidents of assault and the payment of moneys by cheque to the in-laws of the deceased. The FIR had referred to the telephone calls which were received both from the father-in-law of the deceased on the morning and from the deceased on two occasions on the same day-a few hours before her body was found. The grant of anticipatory bail in such a serious offence would operate to obstruct the investigation. The FIR by a father who had suffered the death of his daughter in these circumstances could not be regarded as engineered to falsely implicate the spouse of the deceased and his family.

(ii) It was necessary to entrust a further investigation of the case to the CBI in exercise of the powers of this Court under Article 142 of the Constitution. The conduct of the investigating authorities from the stage of arriving at the scene of occurrence to the filing of the charge-sheet did not inspire confidence in the robustness of the process. A perusal of the charge-sheet evinces a perfunctory rendition of the investigating authorities duty by a bare reference to the facts and the presumption under Section 304B of the IBC (sic Indian Penal Code) when the death occurs within seven years of the marriage. The stance taken by the Deputy Superintendent of Police in the Counter Affidavit, filed a few days after forwarding the charge-sheet, travels beyond the scope of the investigation recorded in the charge-sheet with respect to the veracity of the suicide note, medical examination of injuries and the past miscarriages of the deceased.

Critical facts of the money trail between the deceased, her father (the informant), and the Accused and the call history of A2, the informant and the deceased were unexplored. No attempt at custodial interrogation of the applicants was made between the issuance of non-bailable warrants and interim protection from arrest by the High Court granted. Upon questioning during the hearing, the Counsel for the State answered that no investigation on the allegation of murder had been conducted. It would indeed be a travesty if this Court were to ignore the glaring deficiencies in the investigation conducted so far, irrespective of the stage of the proceedings or the nature of the question before this Court. The status of the Accused as propertied and wealthy persons of influence in Agra and the conduct of the investigation thus far diminishes this Court's faith in directing a further investigation by the same authorities. The cause of justice would not be served if the Court were to confine the scope of its examination to the wisdom of granting anticipatory bail and ignore the possibility of a trial being concluded on the basis of a deficient investigation at best or a biased one at worst.

NINE

RASHMI CHOPRA AND ORS. VS. THE STATE OF UTTAR PRADESH AND ORS., 2019

Hon'ble Judges/Coram:

Ashok Bhushan and K.M. Joseph, JJ.

Relevant Sections:

CRIMINAL MATTERS - MATTERS FOR/AGAINST QUASHING OF CRIMINAL PROCEEDINGS

No. of pdf Pages of the Original Judgment: 14

Equivalent Citation:

2020(3)ACR2323, 2019(201)AIC100, AIR2019SC2297, 2019 (2) ALD(Crl.) 201 (SC), 2019(4) ALJ 344, 2019 (109) ACC 275, 2019(3)BomCR(Cri)259, 128(2019)CLT659, 2019CriLJ3450, 2019(2)Crimes301(SC), II(2019)DMC225SC, 2019(3)HLR488, ILR2019(2)Kerala361, 2019(2)JKJ105[SC], 2019(2)KLT1053, 2019(3)MLJ(Crl)229, 2019(3)RCR(Criminal)97, 2019(4)RLW2932(SC), 2019(7)SCALE152, (2019)15SCC357, 2019 (8) SCJ 499 MANU/SC/0625/2019

Case Note:

Criminal - Quashing of complaint - Entitlement - Section 498A of Indian Penal Code, 1860 (IPC) and Section 3/4 of Dowry Prohibition Act, 1961 (D.P. Act) and Section 482 of Code of Criminal Procedure, 1973 (CrPC) - Present appeals had been filed challenging judgment of High Court by which application under Section 482 of CrPC filed by Appellants praying for quashing the complaint and proceedings in Complaint Case had been dismissed - Whether High Court failed to exercise jurisdiction under Section 482 of CrPC as proceedings are nothing but abuse of the process of the court.

Facts:

Nayan Chopra, son of Rashmi Chopra and Rajesh Chopra got married with Vanshika Bobal, daughter of Respondent No. 2. All the Appellants are family members of Nayan Chopra. On 28.04.2012, Vanshika and Nayan Chopra left for the U.S.A. On or about November, 2013, Vanshika and Nayan Chopra separated. On 23.10.2014, an application was filed by Nayan Chopra in the Circuit Court, Michigan, USA, seeking divorce. On the basis of the application of divorce by Nayan Chopra, the Circuit Court, Michigan gave a judgment of divorce on 24th February, 2016. The judgment of divorce made provisions for alimony, pension benefits and retirement benefits, life insurance, property settlement and provision in lieu of dower, mutual release of claims and other provisions. The application under Section 156(3) of CrPC filed by Respondent No. 2 was treated as a complaint and registered as Complaint on which the learned Judicial Magistrate, issued a summoning order summoning the Appellants Under Sections 498A, 323, 504, 506 of IPC and Section 3/4 of DP Act. The Appellants filed an application under Section 482 of CrPC in the High Court praying for quashing the complaint and proceedings in Complaint Case. Prayer of the Appellants to quash the complaint and proceedings has been refused. Aggrieved against the judgment of the High Court, these appeals have been filed.

Ratio Decidendi:

Complaint filed by father of woman subjected to cruelty is maintainable

Hon'ble Apex Court Held, while dismissing/ allowing the appeal:

Held, while allowing the appeal in part

1. In the present case, there are two sets of allegations. One set of allegations of offence under Section 498A and Section 3/4 of D.P. Act and second set of allegations are allegations made for offences Under Sections 323, 504 and 506 of IPC.

2. Allegations Under Sections 323, 504 and 506 has been made citing the incident dated 08.11.2014.

3. This Court in Rakhi Mishra's case has also laid down that, High Court in exceptional circumstances can exercise power under Section 482 of CrPC, when a prima facie case is not made out against the accused.

4. The criminal prosecution can be allowed to proceed only when a prima facie offence is disclosed. This Court has observed that, judicial process is a solemn proceeding which cannot be allowed to be converted into an instrument of oppression or harassment. If High Court finds that proceedings deserve to be quashed in parameters as laid down by this Court in State of Haryana v. Bhajan Lal, High court shall not hesitate in exercise of jurisdiction under Section 482 of CrPC to quash the proceedings.

5. Complaint has been filed by the Respondent No. 2 before the C.J.M., on 10th May, 2015, before which date, the petition for divorce has already been filed by Nayan Chopra on before the Circuit Court for the County of Kalamazoo Family Division, Michigan. It is on the record that at the time of filing of the complaint Vanishka Bobal was living at Canada whereas Nayan Chopra was living at U.S.A. Both were separately living. It was pleaded in the application for divorce that husband and wife had separated on or around November, 2013. It is on the record that, on the day criminal complaint was filed in the Court of C.J.M. by Respondent No. 2, neither Vanishka was in India nor she was in India at the time when statements were recorded in complaint of complainant as well as his two witnesses. The complaint is not by Vanishka but it has been filed by father of Vanishka, Respondent No. 2. In the divorce application filed in the State of Michigan, Vanishka Bobal was represented by her attorney. The divorce was granted with orders relating to alimony, pension benefits and retirement benefits, life insurance, property settlement and provision in lieu of dower, mutual release of claims on 24th February, 2016.

6. Decree of divorce between Nayan Chopra and Vanshika shall not wipe out any criminal offence, which has been committed within the meaning of IPC or D.P. Act and the criminal offence committed in jurisdictional court has to be examined despite the divorce decree having been granted.

7. Regarding allegations in the complaint pertaining to Section 498A and Section 3/4 of D.P. Act. A perusal of the complaint indicates that, the allegations against the Appellants for offence under Section 498A and Section 3/4 of D.P. Act are general and sweeping. No specific incident dates or details of any incident has been mentioned in the complaint. The complaint having been filed after proceeding for divorce was initiated by Nayan Chopra in State of Michigan, where Vanshika participated and divorce was ultimately granted. A few months after filing of the divorce petition, the complaint has been filed in the Court of C.J.M. The sequence of the events and facts and circumstances of the case leads present Court to

conclude that, the complaint under Section 498A and Section 3/4 of D.P. Act have been filed as counter blast to divorce petition proceeding in State of Michigan by Nayan Chopra.

8. There being no specific allegation regarding any one of the applicants except common general allegation against everyone i.e. "they started harassing the daughter of the applicant demanding additional dowry of one crore" and the fact that all relatives of the husband, namely, father, mother, brother, mother's sister and husband of mother's sister have been roped in clearly indicate that, application under Section 156(3) of CrPC was filed with a view to harass the applicants. Further, prior to filing of the application under Section 156(3) of CrPC, there was no complaint at any point of time by the girl or her father making allegation of demand of any dowry by any one of the applicants. When both Nayan Chopra and Vanshika started living separately since November, 2013, had there been any dowry demand or harassment, the girl would have given complaint to Police or any other authority. Further, in the divorce proceedings at Michigan, U.S.A., parties have agreed for dividing their properties including gifts given at marriage but no complaint was made in those proceedings regarding harassment by her husband or his family members.

9. The above judgment in divorce proceedings indicates that, Nayan Chopra and Vanshika have settled all issues between them including division of properties at the time when divorce proceedings were in progress at Michigan and both the parties were not in India, the complaint under Section 156(3) of CrPC had been filed making allegation under Section 498A of IPC and the Dowry Prohibition Act only to harass and put pressure on the applicants.

10. Section 498A provides for an offence when husband or the relative of the husband, subject her to cruelty. There is nothing in Section 498A, which may indicate that, when a woman is subjected to cruelty, a complaint has to be filed necessarily by the women so subjected. A perusal of Section 498A, indicates that the provision does not contemplate that complaint for offence under Section 498A should be filed only by women, who is subjected to cruelty by husband or his relative. Complaint filed by Respondent No. 2, the father of Vanshika cannot be said to be not maintainable on this ground.

11. Insofar as the offence under Section 498A and Section 3/4 of D.P. Act is concerned, present is a case, which is covered by Category 7 as enumerated by State of Haryana v. Bhajan Lal and the High Court erred in

refusing to exercise its jurisdiction under Section 482 of CrPC. In so far as allegations against Rajesh Chopra pertaining to Sections 323, 504 and 506 of IPC is concerned, there were specific allegations, which were also supported by the complainant and his two witnesses in the evidence. At this stage, this Court cannot pronounce as to whether any incident as alleged by the complainant happened on 8th November, 2014 or alleged as offence by Respondent No. 2 or offence as alleged was committed by Rajesh Chopra or not. Insofar as complaint pertaining to offence under Sections 323, 504 and 506 of IPC against Rajesh Chopra is concerned, said complaint shall be proceeded with and the order is upheld to the above extent only, i.e., summoning of Rajesh Chopra under Sections 323, 504 and 506 of IPC.

TEN

RAHNA JALAL VS. STATE OF KERALA AND ORS., 2020

Hon'ble Judges/Coram:

Dr. D.Y. Chandrachud, Indu Malhotra and Indira Banerjee, JJ.

Relevant Sections:

CRIMINAL MATTERS - CRIMINAL MATTERS RELATING TO BAIL/ INTERIM BAIL/ANTICIPATORY BAIL AND AGAINST SUSPENSION OF SENTENCE

No. of pdf Pages of the Original Judgment: 8

Equivalent Citation:

AIR2021SC225, 2021(4)ALD213, 2021(3)BLJ35, 2021(2)Crimes136(SC), 2021(5)CTC99, 2021(1)HLR311, ILR2021(1)Kerala161, 2021 (1) KHC 97, 2021(1)KLJ775, 2021(1)KLT176, 2021(1)RLW220(SC), (2021)1SCC733 MANU/SC/ 0982/2020

Case Note:

Criminal - Anticipatory bail - Grant of - Sections 34 and 498-A of Indian Penal Code, 1860 - Second Respondent lodged first information report, complaining of offences under provisions of Section 498-A read with Section 34 of Code and Muslim Women Act, 2019 - FIR contains allegation that Appellant's son pronounced talaq three times at their house - High Court was moved with application for anticipatory bail by Petitioners - Single Judge of High Court declined to grant anticipatory bail - Hence, present appeal - Whether Appellants entitled for anticipatory bail.

Facts:

The second Respondent lodged a first information report, complaining of offences under the provisions of Section 498-A read with Section 34 of the Indian Penal Code and the Muslim Women (Protection of Rights on Marriage) Act, 2019. The FIR contains an allegation that the Appellant's son pronounced talaq three times at their house. Following this, it has been stated, the Appellant's son entered into a second marriage. The High Court was moved with an application for anticipatory bail by both Petitioners. The Single Judge of the High Court declined to grant anticipatory bail.

Hon'ble Apex Court Held, while dismissing/ allowing the appeal:

Held, while allowing the appeal:

(i) On a true and harmonious construction of Section 438 of Code of Criminal Procedure and Section 7(c) of the Act, there was no bar on granting anticipatory bail for an offence committed under the Act, provided that the competent court must hear the married Muslim woman who has made the complaint before granting the anticipatory bail. It would be at the discretion of the court to grant ad-interim relief to the Accused during the pendency of the anticipatory bail application, having issued notice to the married Muslim woman.

(ii) By the order of this Court, interim protection from arrest had been granted to the Appellant. The primary allegation which was pressed in aid to deny anticipatory bail is the pronouncement of triple talaq by the spouse of the second Respondent. An offence under the Act was by the Muslim man who had pronounced talaq upon his spouse, and not the Appellant, who was the mother-in-law of the second Respondent. Though, the State had adverted to the allegations under Section 498A of the Code of Criminal Procedure to oppose the grant of bail, having regard to the vague and general nature of those allegations in the FIR, bereft of details, the Appellant (whose son is in a marital relationship with the second Respondent) should not be denied the benefit of the grant of anticipatory bail. It must also be noted that the Judicial Magistrate First Class-I, while deciding the second Respondent's application under Section 23 of the Protection of Women from Domestic Violence Act, 2005 did not find any substance in the allegations against the Appellant.

ELEVEN

S. VANITHA VS. THE DEPUTY COMMISSIONER, BENGALURU URBAN DISTRICT AND ORS., 2020

Hon'ble Judges/Coram:

Dr. D.Y. Chandrachud, Indu Malhotra and Indira Banerjee, JJ.

Relevant Sections:

FAMILY LAW MATTER - ADOPTION AND MAINTENANCE MATTERS

No. of pdf Pages of Original Petition: 17

Equivalent Citation:

2021(1)ADJ347, 2021(217)AIC20, AIR2021SC177, 2021(2)ALD17, 2021 (144) ALR 762, 2021 (1) CCC 1 , 2021(1)Crimes53(SC), I(2021)DMC3SC, (2021)1GLR784, 2021(1)HLR98, 2021(1)ICC53, 2021(1)J.L.J.R.353, 2021(1)JLJ376, 2021(3)KarLJ347, 2020 (6) KHC 749, 2021(1)KLJ609, 2021(1)KLT80, 2021(5)MhLj39, (2021)1MLJ431, 2021(2)MPLJ584, 2021(1)PLJR373, (2021)201PLR117, 2021 151 RD116 MANU/SC/0943/2020

Case Note:

Family - Eviction - Shared household - Section 23 (2) of Senior Citizen Act 2007 and Section 2 of Protection of Women from Domestic Violence Act

2005 - Second and Third Respondents filed application under provisions of Maintenance and Welfare of Parents and Senior Citizens Act 2007 and inter alia, sought Appellant and her daughter's eviction from residential house - Assistant Commissioner, and Deputy Commissioner in appeal, allowed application and directed Appellant to vacate suit premises - Aggrieved by this order, Appellant pursued writ proceeding before Single Judge, and in appeal before Division Bench of High Court - Division Bench held that suit premises belonged to mother-in-law (Second Respondent) of Appellant - Division Bench upheld Order of Deputy Commissioner, and directed Appellant to vacate suit premises - Hence, present appeal - Whether impugned order of ousting Appellant as daughter-in-law and minor daughter was suffer from any infirmity.

Facts:

The Second and Third Respondents filed an application under the provisions of the Maintenance and Welfare of Parents and Senior Citizens Act 2007, and inter alia, sought the Appellant and her daughter's eviction from a residential house. The Assistant Commissioner, and the Deputy Commissioner in appeal, allowed the application under the Senior Citizens Act 2007 and directed the Appellant to vacate the suit premises. Aggrieved by this order, the Appellant unsuccessfully pursued a writ proceeding before a Single Judge, and in appeal before a Division Bench of the High Court of Karnataka. The Division Bench held that the suit premises belonged to the mother-in-law (the Second Respondent) of the Appellant and the remedy of the Appellant for maintenance and shelter lies only against her estranged husband (the Fourth Respondent). The Division Bench upheld the Order of the Deputy Commissioner, and directed the Appellant to vacate the suit premises.

Ratio Decidendi:

The right of a woman to secure a residence order in respect of a shared household cannot be defeated by the simple expedient of securing an order of eviction by adopting the summary procedure under the Senior Citizens Act 2007.

Hon'ble Apex Court Held, while dismissing/ allowing the appeal:

Held, while allowing the appeal:

(i) Both pieces of legislation are intended to deal with salutary aspects of public welfare and interest. The PWDV Act 2005 was intended to deal with the problems of domestic violence which, as the Statements of Objects and

Reasons sets out, is widely prevalent but has remained largely invisible in the public domain. The Statements of Objects and Reasons indicates that while Section 498A of the Indian Penal Code created a penal offence out of a woman's subjection to cruelty by her husband or relative, the civil law did not address its phenomenon in its entirety. Hence, consistent with the provisions of Articles 14, 15 and 21 of the Constitution, Parliament enacted a legislation which would provide for a remedy under the civil law which is intended to protect the woman from being victims of domestic violence and to prevent the occurrence of domestic violence in the society. The ambit of the Bill indicates that a significant object of the legislation is to provide for and recognize the rights of women to secure housing and to recognize the right of a woman to reside in a matrimonial home or a shared household, whether or not she has any title or right in the shared household. Allowing the Senior Citizens Act 2007 to have an overriding force and effect in all situations, irrespective of competing entitlements of a woman to a right in a shared household within the meaning of the PWDV Act 2005, would defeat the object and purpose which the Parliament sought to achieve in enacting the latter legislation. The law protecting the interest of senior citizens is intended to ensure that they are not left destitute, or at the mercy of their children or relatives. Equally, the purpose of the PWDV Act 2005 cannot be ignored by a sleight of statutory interpretation. Both sets of legislations have to be harmoniously construed. Hence the right of a woman to secure a residence order in respect of a shared household cannot be defeated by the simple expedient of securing an order of eviction by adopting the summary procedure under the Senior Citizens Act 2007.

(ii) On construing the provisions of Sub-section (2) of Section 23 of the Senior Citizen Act 2007, it was evident that it applies to a situation where a senior citizen had a right to receive maintenance out of an estate and such estate or part thereof is transferred. On the other hand, the Appellant's simple plea was that the suit premises constitute her shared household within the meaning of Section 2 of the PWDV Act 2005. The series of transactions which took place in respect of the property, the spouse of the Appellant purchased it in his own name a few months before the marriage but subsequently sold it, after a few years, under a registered sale deed at the same price to his father (the father-in-law of the Appellant), who in turn gifted it to his spouse i.e. the mother-in-law of the Appellant after divorce proceedings were instituted by the Fourth Respondent. Parallel to this, the

Appellant had instituted proceedings of dowry harassment against her mother-in-law and her estranged spouse and her spouse had instituted divorce proceedings. The Appellant had also filed proceedings for maintenance against the Fourth Respondent and the divorce proceedings are pending. It is subsequent to these events, that the Second and Third Respondents instituted an application under the Senior Citizens Act 2007. The fact that specific proceedings under the PWDV Act 2005 had not been instituted when the application under the Senior Citizens Act, 2007 was filed, should not lead to a situation where the enforcement of an order of eviction deprives her from pursuing her claim of entitlement under the law. The inability of a woman to access judicial remedies may, as this case exemplifies, be a consequence of destitution, ignorance or lack of resources. Even otherwise, recourse to the summary procedure contemplated by the Senior Citizen Act 2007 was not available for the purpose of facilitating strategies that are designed to defeat the claim of the Appellant in respect of a shared household. A shared household would have to be interpreted to include the residence where the Appellant had been jointly residing with her husband. Merely because the ownership of the property has been subsequently transferred to her in-laws (Second and Third Respondents) or that her estranged spouse (Fourth Respondent) was now residing separately, was no ground to deprive the Appellant of the protection that was envisaged under the PWDV Act 2005.

(iii) The claim of the Appellant that the premises constitute a shared household within the meaning of the PWDV Act 2005 would have to be determined by the appropriate forum. The claim could not simply be obviated by evicting the Appellant in exercise of the summary powers entrusted by the Senior Citizens Act 2007. The Second and Third Respondents were at liberty to make a subsequent application under Section 10 of the Senior Citizens Act 2007 for alteration of the maintenance allowance, before the appropriate forum.

TWELVE

NAGABHUSHAN VS. THE STATE OF KARNATAKA, 2021

Hon'ble Judges/ Coram:
Dr. D.Y. Chandrachud and M.R. Shah, JJ.

Relevant Sections:

CRIMINAL MATTERS - APPEAL Under Section 2 OF THE SUPREME COURT (ENLARGEMENT OF JURISDICTION) ACT

No. of pdf Pages of the Original Judgment: 13

Equivalent Citation:

2021(220)AIC237, AIR2021SC1290, 2021 (2) ALD(Crl.) 263 (SC), 2021 (115) ACC 679, 2021CriLJ1606, I(2021)DMC555SC, 2021(2)JKJ113[SC], 2021(2)KCCR1057, 2021(2)N.C.C.1, 2021(2)RCR(Criminal)289, (2021)5SCC222, 2021 (2) SCJ 740 MANU/SC/0164/2021

Case Note:

Criminal - Conviction - Sections 34, 302 and 498A of the Indian Penal Code, 1860 (IPC) - Section 378 of the Code of Criminal Procedure, 1973 (CrPC) - High Court vide impugned judgment reversed Trial Court's judgment of acquittal - Appellant contended that High Court committed grave error in reversing the well-reasoned judgment by the learned trial Court - High Court contended to have exceeded jurisdiction vested in it under Section 378, CrPC and wrongly relied on dying declarations - Whether the conviction of Appellant in the above circumstances, liable to be set aside?

Facts:

As per the case of the prosecution, Appellant married to deceased used to subject her with mental cruelty and there was demand of dowry from her parents. On the relevant date, Appellant took up quarrel with deceased and at that time, he took kerosene and poured the same on her and lit the fire. The deceased was taken to the hospital. Statement of deceased was recorded in an interval of two days. FIR was registered and charge sheet was filed against all the Accused person. High Court vide impugned judgment allowed appeal preferred by the Respondent-State to reverse the judgment and order of acquittal passed by the Trial Court insofar as the Appellant-original Accused No. 1 was concerned and consequently convicted the Appellant. In respect of Accused Nos. 2 and 3 High Court confirmed the judgment and order of acquittal. Trial Court had acquitted after appreciating evidence and not believing the dying declaration after finding contradictions in two dying declarations. Appellant filed the present appeal against the impugned judgment of the High Court.

Hon'ble Apex Court Held, while dismissing/ allowing the appeal:

Held, while dismissing the Appeal:

High Court has specifically observed and held that the finding recorded by the learned trial Court discarding and/or not believing the dying declaration (Exhibit P5) is perverse and contrary to the evidence on record. The High Court has given cogent reasons while believing dying declaration (Exhibit P5) and has also considered in detail what is stated in the later dying declaration (Exhibit P5), the medical evidence and the injuries sustained by the deceased. Therefore, as such, the High Court has not committed any error in re-appreciating the entire evidence on record and thereafter interfering with the judgment and order of acquittal passed by the learned trial Court, having found the finding recorded by the learned trial Court perverse.

In the present case there are two dying declarations, (i) Exhibit P5 and (ii) Exhibit D2. The High Court in the impugned judgment and order has given cogent reasons to rely upon and believe the second dying declaration-Exhibit P5. The High Court has also taken note of the fact that the second dying declaration is reliable and the version in the second dying declaration is supported by the circumstances, namely, the injuries sustained by the deceased; no stove was found at the place of occurrence. The High Court has also taken note of the fact that in the second dying declaration, the deceased has explained her first statement that it was a case of accident and she categorically stated in the second dying declaration that at the time when she gave first statement that it was a case of accident, she was given threats by the Appellant herein-original Accused No. 1 that he will kill her children also. She also stated in the second dying declaration that after her parents came, she got the courage to tell the truth. Therefore, as such, the High Court rightly believed the second dying declaration-Exhibit P5.

No reason to interfere with the impugned judgment and order of conviction passed by the High Court. The appeal accordingly dismissed.

THIRTEEN

KRISHNAVENI RAI VS. PANKAJ RAI AND ORS., 2020

Hon'ble Judges/Coram:

Indira Banerjee and M.R. Shah, JJ.

Relevant Sections:

Family - Maintenance - Validity of marriage - Section 125 of Code of Criminal Procedure, 1973 and Section 15 of Hindu Marriage Act, 1955

No. of pdf Pages of the Original Judgment: 8

Equivalent Citation:

AIR2020SC1156, 2020(4)ALD138, 2020 (2) ALD(Crl.) 180 (SC), 2020(2)ALT91, 2021 (1) ALT (Crl.) 499 (A.P.), 2020(3)BLJ263, 2020(2)CTC359, I(2020)DMC716SC, 2021GLH(1)237, 2020(1)HLR870, 2020(3)J.L.J.R.237, 2020(1)JCC712, 2020(2)JKJ280[SC], 2020(2)JLJ613, 2020 (2) KHC 48, 2020(1)KLJ934, 2020(2)KLT256, 2020(II)OLR224, 2020(3)PLJR169, 2020(2)RCR(Criminal)154, 2020(2)RLW1005(SC), (2020)11SCC253, 2020(2)UC997 MANU/SC/0215/2020

Case Note:

Family - Maintenance - Validity of marriage - Section 125 of Code of Criminal Procedure, 1973 and Section 15 of Hindu Marriage Act, 1955 - Appellant's first marriage was dissolved by decree of divorce and appeal preferred against said decree of divorce after lapse of period of limitation which was condoned - Said appeal was, however, formally dismissed as withdrawn - Thereafter, Appellant married the Respondent No. 1 which also did not work - Appellant lodged complaint against Respondent No. 1

under Sections 406, 498A and 500 of Code - Appellant filed application under Section 125 of Code for maintenance - Respondent No. 1 filed application for discharge, from criminal proceedings initiated against him, which was dismissed - Respondent No. 1 filed criminal Revision Petition against said order - Metropolitan Sessions Judge allowed Criminal Revision Petition and discharged Respondent No. 1 - In meanwhile, Additional Metropolitan Sessions Judge, dismissed application filed by Appellant, claiming maintenance under Section 125 of Code -Appellant filed revision petition in High Court discharging Respondent No. 1 - High Court suspended said order of discharge - Respondent No. 1, filed petition in High Court for quashing of criminal proceedings against him - Said criminal proceedings were quashed on ground that marriage of Appellant with Respondent No. 1, solemnised during pendency of appeal from decree of dissolution of Appellant's marriage with her first husband, was null and void - Revision Petition filed by Appellant against order passed by Additional Metropolitan Sessions Judge dismissing application under Section 125 of Code was also dismissed on same ground on which Criminal proceedings against Respondent No. 1 had been quashed - Hence, present appeal - Whether marriage of Appellant with Respondent No. 1, solemnised during pendency of appeal from decree of dissolution of Appellant's marriage with her first husband, was null and void.

Facts:

The Appellant's first marriage was dissolved by decree of divorce and appeal preferred against said decree of divorce after lapse of period of limitation which was condoned. The said appeal was, however, formally dismissed as withdrawn. Thereafter, the Appellant married the Respondent No. 1, unfortunately, the Appellant's second marriage also did not work. The Appellant had alleged that the Respondent No. 1 subjected the Appellant to harassment and cruelty and even threw her out of the matrimonial home. The Appellant lodged a complaint against the Respondent No. 1 under Sections 406, 498A and 500 of Indian Penal Code. The Appellant filed an application under Section 125 the Code of Criminal Procedure for maintenance. The Respondent No. 1 filed an application under Section 239 for Code of Criminal Procedure for discharge, from the proceedings initiated pursuant to FIR which was dismissed. The Respondent No. 1 filed a criminal Revision Petition in the Court of the Metropolitan Sessions Judge, challenging the said order of Additional Chief Metropolitan Magistrate, rejecting the application of the Respondent No. 1 for discharge. The

Metropolitan Sessions Judge, allowed the Criminal Revision Petition and discharged the Respondent No. 1 from the proceedings Under Section 406, 498A and 500 of the Indian Penal Code. In the meanwhile, the Additional Metropolitan Sessions Judge, dismissed the application filed by the Appellant, claiming maintenance under Section 125 Code of Criminal Procedure. The Appellant filed a Criminal Revision Petition in the High Court inter alia challenging the order discharging the Respondent No. 1 from the proceeding under Sections 406, 498A and 500 of the Indian Penal Code and also made an application for suspension of the said order of discharge. By an order, the High Court suspended the said order of discharge. The Respondent No. 1, on the other hand, filed a petition under Section 482 of the Code of Criminal Procedure, for quashing of the criminal proceedings against him. The said criminal proceedings were quashed on the ground that the marriage of the Appellant with the Respondent No. 1, solemnised during the pendency of an appeal from the decree of dissolution of the Appellant's marriage with her first husband, was null and void. The Criminal Revision Petition filed by the Appellant against the order passed by the Additional Metropolitan Sessions Judge dismissing the application under Section 125 of the Code of Criminal Procedure was also dismissed by an order on the same ground on which the Criminal proceedings against the Respondent No. 1 had been quashed.

Hon'ble Apex Court Held, while dismissing/ allowing the appeal:

Held, while allowing the appeal:

(i) The bar, if any, under Section 15 of the Hindu Marriage Act applies only if there is an appeal filed within the period of limitation, and not afterwards upon condonation of delay in filing an appeal unless of course, the decree of divorce is stayed or there is an interim order of Court, restraining the parties or any of them from remarrying during the pendency of the appeal.

(ii) The appeal was infructuous for all practical purposes, from the inception, since the Appellant's ex-husband had lawfully remarried after expiry of the period of limitation for filing an appeal, there being no appeal till then.

(iii) It could never have been the legislative intent that a marriage validly contracted after the divorce and after expiry of the period of limitation to file an appeal from the decree of divorce should rendered void on the filing of a belated appeal. If the marriage of the Appellant's ex-husband was a valid marriage in law recognizing that he had no living spouse, the subsequent re-marriage of the Appellant could also not be void. We are in full agreement with the view of this Court in Leela Gupta that the effect of the prohibition against one of the parties from contracting a second marriage for a certain period is not to nullify the divorce and continue the dissolved marriage, as if the same were subsisting.

(iv)The judgment and order under appeal confirming the order dismissing the application under Section 125 of Code by relying on the order in Criminal Petition could not be sustained.

FOURTEEN

Preet Pal Singh Vs. The State of Uttar Pradesh and Ors., 2020

Hon'ble Judges/Coram:

Arun Mishra and Indira Banerjee, JJ.

Relevant Sections:

CRIMINAL MATTERS - CRIMINAL MATTERS RELATING TO CANCELLATION TO BAIL

No. of pdf Pages of the Original Judgment: 8

Equivalent Citation:

2020(3)ACR2128, 2021(2)ACR2012, 2020(8)ADJ612, 2020(214)AIC129, AIR2020SC3995, 2020 (2) ALD(Crl.) 707 (SC), 2020 (113) ACC 679, 2020(5)BLJ355, 2020(3)Crimes147(SC), I(2021)DMC45SC, 2020(3)J.L.J.R.421, 2020(4)JKJ123[SC], 2020(3)MLJ(Crl)633, 2020(3)PLJR371, 2020(4)RCR(Criminal)848, (2020)8SCC645, 2020(2)UC1281 MANU/SC/0591/2020

Case Note:

Criminal - Suspension of sentence - Validity of - Sections 304B, 406 and 498A of Indian Penal Code, 1860, Section 389 of Code of Criminal Procedure, 1973 and Sections 3 and 4 of Dowry Prohibition Act, 1961 - Sessions Court convicted Respondent No.2 for offences under Sections 304B, 498A and 406 of Code and Sections 3 and 4 of Act - Being aggrieved by conviction and sentence, Respondent No. 2 filed appeal in High Court - After filing appeal, Respondent No. 2 filed application inter alia praying that he be enlarged on bail, during pendency of appeal - High Court granted bail to Respondent No. 2 by staying execution of sentences of imprisonment - Hence, present appeal - Whether High Court erred in granting bail to Respondent No. 2 by staying execution of sentences of imprisonment.

Facts:

The Sessions Court convicted Respondent No. 2 for offences under Sections 304B, 498A and 406 of the Indian Penal Code (IPC) and Sections 3 and 4 of the Dowry Prohibition Act, 1961 by staying execution of the sentences of imprisonment. Being aggrieved by the conviction and sentence, the Respondent No. 2 filed an appeal in the High Court. After filing the appeal, the Respondent No. 2 filed application inter alia praying that he be enlarged on bail, during the pendency of the aforesaid appeal. The said application had been allowed. The High Court granted bail to the Respondent No. 2, husband of the deceased victim, convicted by a judgment of the Additional District and Sessions Judge/Special Judge (EC Act), for offences under Sections 304B, 498A and 406 of the Indian Penal Code (IPC) and Sections 3 and 4 of the Dowry Prohibition Act, 1961 by staying execution of the sentences of imprisonment.

Hon'ble Apex Court Held, while dismissing/ allowing the appeal:

Held, while allowing the appeal:

(i) It was nobody's case that the death of the victim was accidental or natural. There was evidence of demand of dowry, which the Trial Court had considered. The death took place within seven or eight months and there was oral evidence of the parents of cruelty and torture immediately preceding the death. There was also evidence of payment to the Respondent-Accused by the victim's brother. The Respondent No. 2 had not been able to demonstrate any apparent and/or obvious illegality or error in the judgment of the Sessions Court, to call for suspension of execution of the sentence.

(ii) In considering an application for suspension of sentence, the Appellate Court was only to examine if there was such patent infirmity in the order of conviction that renders the order of conviction prima facie erroneous. Where there was evidence that had been considered by the Trial Court, it was not open to a Court considering application under Section 389 to re-assess and/or re-analyze the same evidence and take a different view, to suspend the execution of the sentence and release the convict on bail.

(iii) It was difficult to appreciate how the High Court could casually have suspended the execution of the sentence and granted bail to the Respondent No. 2 without recording any reasons, with the casual observation of force in the argument made on behalf of the Appellant before the High Court, that was, the Respondent No. 2. In effect, at the stage of an application under Section 389 of the Code of Criminal Procedure, the High Court found merit in the submission that the brother of the victim not having been examined, the contention of the Respondent No. 2, being the Appellant before the High Court, that the amount was taken as a loan was not refuted, ignoring the evidence relied upon by the Sessions Court, including the oral evidence of the victim's parents.

(iv) From the evidence of the Prosecution witnesses, it transpires that the Appellant had spent money beyond his financial capacity, at the wedding of the victim and had even gifted an car. The hapless parents were hoping against hope that there would be an amicable settlement. Even as late the brother of the victim paid amount to the Respondent No. 2. The failure to lodge an FIR complaining of dowry and harassment before the death of the victim, was inconsequential. The parents and other family members of the victim obviously would not want to precipitate a complete breakdown of the marriage by lodging an FIR against the Respondent No. 2 and his parents, while the victim was alive.

(v) The impugned order of the High Court was set aside and the Respondent No. 2 was directed to surrender for being taken into custody.

ϸϸϸ

FIFTEEN

NALLAPAREDDY SRIDHAR REDDY VS. THE STATE OF ANDHRA PRADESH AND ORS., 2020

Hon'ble Judges/Coram:

Dr. D.Y. Chandrachud and Hrishikesh Roy, JJ.

Relevant Sections:

Criminal - Additional charges - Framing of - Section 216 of Code of Criminal Procedure, 1973 and Sections 406 and 420 of Indian Penal Code, 1860 Section 498A of Indian Penal Code, 1860 along with Sections 3 and 4 of Dowry Prohibition Act 1961.

No. of pdf Pages of the Original Judgment: 10

Equivalent Citation:

2020(211)AIC191, 2020(211)AIC191, AIR2020SC753, 2020 (1) ALD(Crl.) 759 (SC), 2020 (112) ACC 850, 2020 (2) ALT (Crl.) 17 (A.P.), 2020CriLJ1792, 2020(1)Crimes198(SC), 2020(1)CTC810, 2020(1)J.L.J.R.363, 2020(1)JKJ219[SC], 2020-2-LW(Crl)326, 2020(1)PLJR407, 2020(1)RCR(Criminal)787, (2020)12SCC467, 2020 (3) SCJ 667, 2020(1)UC30 MANU/SC/0057/2020

Case Note:

Criminal - Additional charges - Framing of - Section 216 of Code of Criminal Procedure, 1973 and Sections 406 and 420 of Indian Penal Code, 1860 - First

Information Report was lodged by fourth Respondent, alleging that Appellant and members of his family had harassed his daughter with demands for money and transfer of land in their names - Trial Court framed charges against Appellant only for offences under Section 498A of Indian Penal Code, 1860 along with Sections 3 and 4 of Dowry Prohibition Act 1961 - Application was filed by Public Prosecutor under Section 216 of Code for framing of additional charges - Trial Court concluded that ingredients for offences under Sections 406 and 420 of Code were not made out and rejected application for framing additional charges - Fourth Respondent filed revision petition before High Court against order of Trial Court - Single Judge of High Court set aside Trial Court's order by holding that Trial Court while rejecting application under Section 216 did not disclose reasons - Hence, present appeal - Whether High Court was right in adding charges under Sections 406 and 420 of Code.

Ratio Decidendi:

The test to be adopted by the court while deciding upon an addition or alteration of a charge is that the material brought on record needs to have a direct link or nexus with the ingredients of the alleged offence.

Facts:

A First Information Report was lodged by the fourth Respondent, who was the father-in-law of the Appellant, alleging that the Appellant and the members of his family had harassed his daughter with demands for money and transfer of land in their names. A charge-sheet was filed against the Appellant and his parents for offences under Section 498A of the Indian Penal Code along with Sections 3 and 4 of the Dowry Prohibition Act 1961. An additional charge-sheet had been filed by the investigating officer implicating the Appellant for crimes under Sections 406 and 420, charges were not framed by the trial judge under those provisions. The Trial Court framed charges against the Appellant only for offences mentioned in the original charge-sheet under Section 498A of Code along with Sections 3 and 4 of the Dowry Prohibition Act. An application was filed by the Public Prosecutor under Section 216 of Code of Criminal Procedure for alteration of charge. The Trial Court after hearing arguments on behalf of both the sides and perusing the material available on record concluded that the ingredients for offences under Sections 406 and 420 Indian Penal Code were not made out and rejected the application for framing additional charges. The fourth Respondent filed a revision petition before the High Court against the above order of the Trial Court. A Single Judge of the High Court allowed the revision petition and set aside the Trial Court's order. The High Court held that the Trial Court while rejecting the application under Section 216 did not disclose the reasons for concluding that the ingredients of Sections 406 and 420 were not attracted and only touched upon the lapses of the prosecution in not seeking an alteration of charges during the course of the trial.

Ratio Decidendi:

The test to be adopted by the court while deciding upon an addition or alteration of a charge is that the material brought on record needs to have a direct link or nexus with the ingredients of the alleged offence.

Hon'ble Apex Court Held, while dismissing/ allowing the appeal:

Held, while dismissing the appeal:

(i) The test adopted by the High Court was correct and in accordance with decisions of this Court. In the counter affidavit filed by the fourth Respondent before this Court, depositions of witneeses and their cross-examination had been annexed. The material on record supports the possibility that the Appellant demanded certain amount from complainant, in order to secure a doctor's job for the complainant's daughter in the foreign country. According to complainant, he borrowed the amount and paid it to the Appellant. Without pronouncing on the probative value of such evidence, there exists sufficient material on record that shows a connection or link with the ingredients of the offences under Sections 406 and 420 of the Indian Penal Code, and the charges sought to be added.

(ii) The veracity of the depositions made by the witnesses was a question of trial and need not be determined at the time of framing of charge. Appreciation of evidence on merit was to be done by the court only after the charges had been framed and the trial had commenced. However, for the purpose of framing of charge the court needs to prima facie determine that there exists sufficient material for the commencement of trial. The High Court had relied upon the materials on record and concluded that the ingredients of the offences under Sections 406 and 420 of the Indian Penal Code were attracted. The High Court had spelt out the reasons that had necessitated the addition of the charge and hence, the impugned order did not warrant any interference.

SIXTEEN

Gurcharan Singh Vs. The State of Punjab, 2020

Hon'ble Judges/Coram:

N.V. Ramana, Surya Kant and Hrishikesh Roy, JJ.

Relevant Sections:

CRIMINAL MATTERS - CRIMINAL MATTERS IN WHICH SENTENCE AWARDED IS UPTO FIVE YEARS

No. of pdf Pages of the Original Judgment: 7

Equivalent Citation:

2021(217)AIC65, AIR2020SC4714, 2020 (2) ALD(Crl.) 1002 (SC), 2021 (114) ACC 687, 2020 (3) ALT (Crl.) 275 (A.P.), 2020(6)BLJ205, 2020(4)Crimes158(SC), 2020(5)JKJ158[SC], 2021-1-LW(Crl)487, 2020(4)MLJ(Crl)220, 2021(I)OLR301, 2020(4)RCR(Criminal)622, 2020(4)RLW3340(SC), (2020)10SCC200, 2021 (1) SCJ 432, 2020(3)UC1443 MANU/SC/0731/2020

Case Note:

Criminal - Abetment - Suicide - Conviction - Sections 107 and 306 of the Indian Penal Code, 1860 (IPC) - Appellant along with his parents acquitted by Trial Court from charges of Sections 304B and 498A, IPC - Conviction of Appellant for abetment however retained - High Court affirmed the view of Trial Court - Hence, the present Appeal - Whether offence of abetment was proved against Appellant to hold him guilty? - Appellant contended no direct evidence of cruelty towards deceased by him or parents-in-law - Court's conclusion contended to be based on conjectures and not upon any substantial evidence.

Facts:

The Appellant along with his parents was charged under Sections 304B and 498A read with Section 34 of the Indian Penal Code. Trial Court ordered acquittal of the parents of Appellant parents. However, the trial Court opined that although no charge of abetment was framed against the husband, he can be convicted for abetting suicide of his wife, under Section 306 Indian Penal Code. High Court also confirmed the view adopted by the Trial Court. Hence, the present appeal.

Ratio Decidendi:

Ingredient of mensrea cannot be assumed to be ostensibly present but has to be visible and conspicuous

Hon'ble Apex Court Held, while dismissing/ allowing the appeal:

Held, while allowing the Appeals:

In all crimes, mensrea has to be established. To prove the offence of abetment, as specified under Section 107 of the Indian Penal Code, the state of mind to commit a particular crime must be visible, to determine the culpability. In order to prove mensrea, there has to be something on record to establish or show that the Appellant herein had a guilty mind and in furtherance of that state of mind, abetted the suicide of the deceased. The ingredient of mensrea cannot be assumed to be ostensibly present but has to be visible and conspicuous. However, what transpires in the present matter is that both the Trial Court as well as the High Court never examined whether Appellant had the mensrea for the crime, he is held to have committed. The conviction of Appellant by the Trial Court as well as the High Court on the theory that the woman with two young kids might have committed suicide, possibly because of the harassment faced by her in the matrimonial house, is not at all borne out by the evidence in the case. Testimonies of the PWs do not show that the wife was unhappy because of the Appellant and she was forced to take such a step on his account.

No overt act or illegal omission seen from the Appellant's side in taking due care of his deceased wife. Evidence does not indicate deceased facing persistent harassment from her husband.

Trial Court and the High Court erred in concluding that the deceased was driven to commit suicide, by the circumstances or atmosphere in the matrimonial home. This is nothing more than an inference, without any material support. Therefore, the same cannot be the basis for sustaining conviction of the Appellant, under Section 306 of the Indian Penal Code.

The Appellant's conviction under Section 306 Indian Penal Code set aside and quashed. The appeal is accordingly, allowed.

SEVENTEEN

SONU VS. SONU YADAV AND ORS., 2021

Hon'ble Judges/Coram:

Dr. D.Y. Chandrachud and M.R. Shah, JJ.

Relevant Sections:

CRIMINAL MATTERS - CRIMINAL MATTERS RELATING TO CANCELLATION TO BAIL

No. of pdf Pages of the Original Judgment: 5

Equivalent Citation:

2021(5)ADJ156, 2021(222)AIC166, AIR2021SC1950, 2021 (2) ALD(Crl.) 228 (SC), 2021 (116) ACC 650, 2021ALLMR(Cri)2667, 2021(2)BomCR(Cri)695, 2021CriLJ2464, (2021)4GLR2931, 2021(2)JKJ414[SC], 2021(2)RCR(Criminal)650, 2021(3)RLW2379(SC), 2021(3)UC1396 MANU/SC/0243/2021

Case Note:

Criminal - Bail - Cancellation of - Sections 304B and 498A of Indian Penal Code, 1860 and Sections 3 and 4 of - First Information Report was registered for offences under Sections 498A and 304-B of Code and Sections 3 and 4 of Act and charge-sheet had been submitted - Bail application filed by first Respondent was rejected by Sessions Judge - High Court was thereafter allowed bail application - Hence, present appeal - Whether High Court erred in grating bail to Respondents.

Facts:

A First Information Report was registered for offences under Sections 498A and 304-B of the Indian Penal Code and Sections 3 and 4 of the Dowry Prohibition Act 1861. A charge-sheet had been submitted for offences alleged under Sections 498-A and 304-B of the Indian Penal Code and Sections 3 and 4 of the Dowry Prohibition Act. The bail application filed by the first Respondent was rejected by the Sessions Judge. The High Court was thereafter moved in a bail application allowed the application.

Hon'ble Apex Court Held, while dismissing/ allowing the appeal:

Held, while allowing the appeal:

(i) It was not in dispute that the first Respondent was married to the sister of the Appellant. She died within a year of the marriage. There were specific allegations in the First Information Report in regard to the demand of dowry, as well as in regard to a phone call being received from the Accused in close proximity to the death of the sister of the Appellant when a demand for additional amounts of money was made. The submission in support of bail recorded by the High Court was that the sister of the Appellant was undergoing treatment for a mental illness. In this context, it was material to note that in the bail application, the plea was that the deceased was suffering from severe headache and was mentally disturbed since the past nine months and that she was taken to a doctor by the first Respondent. A copy of the medical prescription, which had been submitted before this Court, would prima facie indicate that there was no serious ailment. The medical prescription of the Ayurvedic doctor and the remedies prescribed belie such a claim. Prima facie, there are serious allegations in the FIR in regard to the harassment suffered by the deceased in close proximity to her death over demands for dowry by the Accused. In view of the provisions of Section 304-B of the Indian Penal Code, as well as the presumption which arises under Section 113-B of the Evidence Act, the High Court was clearly not justified in granting bail.

(ii) In the earlier part of this judgment, this court had extracted the lone sentence in the order of the High Court which is intended to display some semblance of reasoning for justifying the grant of bail. The sentence which we have extracted earlier contains an omnibus amalgam of the entire facts and circumstances of the case, submissions of Counsel for the parties, the nature of offence, evidence and complicity of Accused. This was followed by an observation that the applicant has made out a case for bail, without expressing any opinion on the merits of the case. This did not constitute the kind of reasoning which was expected of a judicial order. The High Court could not be oblivious, in a case such as the present, of the seriousness of the alleged offence, where a woman had met an unnatural end within a year of marriage. The seriousness of the alleged offence had to be evaluated in the backdrop of the allegation that she was being harassed for dowry and that a telephone call was received from the Accused in close-proximity to the time of death, making a demand. There were specific allegations of harassment against the Accused on the ground of dowry. An order without reasons was fundamentally contrary to the norms which guide the judicial process. The administration of criminal justice by the High Court could not be reduced to a mantra containing a recitation of general observations. That there had been a judicious application of mind by the judge who is deciding an application under Section 439 of the Code of Criminal Procedure must emerge from the quality of the reasoning which was embodied in the order granting bail. While the reasons may be brief, it was the quality of the reasons which matters the most. That was because the reasons in a judicial order unravel the thought process of a trained judicial mind. The reasons indicated in the judgment of the High Court in this case were becoming increasingly familiar in matters which come to this Court. It was time that such a practice was discontinued and that the reasons in support of orders granting bail comport with a judicial process which brings credibility to the administration of criminal justice.

(iii) Therefore, set aside the impugned judgment and order of the Single Judge of the High Court granting bail to the first Respondent.

EIGHTEEN

SAMAUL S.K. VS. THE STATE OF JHARKHAND AND ORS., 2021

Hon'ble Judges/Coram:

Sanjay Kishan Kaul and Hrishikesh Roy, JJ.

Relevant sections:

CRIMINAL MATTERS - MATTERS RELATING TO HARASSMENT, CRUELTY TO WOMAN FOR DOWRY, DOWRY DEATH, EVE-TEASING, DOMESTIC VIOLENCE ETC.

No. of pdf Pages of the Original Judgment : 3

Equivalent Citation:

2021(226)AIC256, 2021 (117) ACC 998, 2021 (3) ALT (Crl.) 382 (A.P.), 2021(5)BLJ225, 2021(3)Crimes314(SC) MANU/SC/0584/2021

Case Note:

Criminal - Dowry demand - Conviction - Section 498A of the Indian Penal Code, 1860 (IPC) - Revision filed challenging conviction dismissed - During the pendency of present petition extension of benefit sought under Probation of Offenders Act, 1958 - Whether Appellant could be granted the benefit as sought?

Facts:

In the instant case alleging dowry demand Appellant was convicted. During the hearing of SLP filed to challenge against order passed in Revision challenging conviction, Appellant sought extension of benefit under Probation of Offenders Act and reduction of sentence. It was though initially declined, Appellant was asked to give adequate compensation to R2 for herself and children besides maintenance as ordered.

Hon'ble Apex Court Held, while dismissing/ allowing the appeal:

Held, while allowing the Appeal:

The object of any criminal jurisprudence is reformative in character and to take care of the victim. It is towards this objective that Section 357 of the Code of Criminal Procedure is enacted in the statute. In the present case, it is one of voluntarily offering the amount albeit to seek a reduction of sentence.

In view of the submission made by the Petitioner requesting for six months' time to make arrangement to deposit/pay the amount, Appellant to deposit amount with the trial court.

Appeal allowed as directed.

PPP

NINETEEN

SATISH CHANDER AHUJA VS. SNEHA AHUJA, 2020

Hon'ble Judges/Coram:

Ashok Bhushan, R. Subhash Reddy and M.R. Shah, JJ.

Relevant Section:

ORDINARY CIVIL MATTERS : MATTERS FOR EVICTION / DISPOSSESSION OTHER THAN RENT CONTROL ACT MATTERS

No. of pdf Pages of the Original Judgment: 45

Equivalent Citation:

2020(11)ADJ158, 2021(218)AIC161, AIR2020SC5397, 2020(6)ALD94, 2021 (145) ALR 218, 2020(6)ALT115, 2020 (3) ALT (Crl.) 368 (A.P.), 2020 6 AWC5516SC, 2020(6)BLJ436, 2020 (4) CCC 449 , 2020(4)Crimes238(SC), III(2020)DMC453SC, 2020GLH(4)416, 2020(3)HLR537, 2021(1)ICC1, ILR2020(4)Kerala421, 2020(4)J.L.J.R.188, 2020(5)JKJ1[SC], 2020(4)JLJ370, 2020 (5) KHC 496, 2020(6)KLT208, (2020)8MLJ48, 2020(4)PLJR211, 2020(4)RCR(Criminal)745, 2020(4)RLW3413(SC), (2021)1SCC414 MANU/SC/0767/2020

Case Note:

Family - 'Shared household' - Meaning thereof - Section 2(s) of the Protection of Women from Domestic Violence Act, 2005 (DV Act) - Right to Residence - Exercise thereof by Daughter-in-law in the property owned by Father-in-law - Determination thereof - Whether definition of shared household under Section 2(s) DV Act, 2005 to be read to mean that shared household can only be that household as household of joint family or wherein husband of the aggrieved person has a share? - Whether the law laid down by Supreme Court in the case of S.R. Batra and Anr. v. TarunaBatra does not lay down a correct law? - Appellant contended suit property exclusively owned by him is not a shared household and his son alongwith his wife were only gratuitous licencees - Respondent on the other hand contended that DV Act, 2005 granted protection and security of residence to woman - Respondent contended to be being in domestic relationship with the Appellant living in the suit property since her marriage and continues to do so till date, and property as shared household

Civil - Right to residence - Shared household - Property belonging to Father-in-law - Decree on Admission - Sustainability thereof - Order XII Rule 6 Code of Civil Procedure, 1908 (CPC) - Section 26 of Protection of Women from Domestic Violence Act, 2005 (DV Act) - Whether the High Court rightly concluded that suit filed by the Appellant could not have been decreed under Order XII Rule 6 Code of Civil Procedure? - Whether, when the Defendant (daughter-in-law) in her written statement pleaded that suit property is her shared household and she has right to residence therein, the Trial Court could have decreed the suit of the Plaintiff without deciding her such claim, permissible to be decided as per Section 26 of the Act, 2005?

Family - Definition of Respondent - 'Adult Male Person' - Domestic Relationship - Aggrieved Person - Section 2(q) of the Protection of Women from Domestic Violence Act, 2005 (DV Act) - Whether the Plaintiff in the suit giving rise to this appeal can be said to be the Respondent as per definition of Section 2(q) of DV Act?

Civil - Impleadment - Domestic Violence - Husband of Aggrieved Party - Order 1 Rule 10 of the Code of Civil Procedure, 1908 (CPC) Whether the husband of aggrieved party (Defendant) is necessary party in the suit filed by the Plaintiff (father-in-law) against the Defendant?

Civil - Jurisdiction - Enforceability and binding effect of Orders - Domestic Violence - Section 19 of the Protection of Women from Domestic Violence Act, 2005 (DV Act) - What is the effect of orders passed Under Section 19 of the Act, 2005 whether interim or final passed in the proceedings initiated in a civil court of competent jurisdiction?

Facts:

Appellant/ Plaintiff purchased property in question. His son got married to the Respondent and after marriage the Respondent started living in the first floor of the property in question along with her husband. Due to marital discord between them, Respondent moved out of the first floor and started staying in the guest room of the ground floor. She later started a separate kitchen in the first floor of the house. Her husband filed a Divorce Petition on the ground of cruelty against the Respondent and said proceeding is still pending. The Respondent after divorce petition was filed, moved an application under Section 12 of DV Act (as Complainant) impleading her husband as Respondent No. 1, Appellant as Respondent No. 2 and her mother in law as Respondent No. 3 alleging them to have caused severe emotional and mental abuses. In the application Respondent prayed for several orders and Trial Court while passing interim order held that Respondents shall not alienate the alleged shared household nor would they dispossess her or their children from the same without orders of a Competent Court. Appellant filed a Suit impleading her daughter-in-law as sole-Defendant for mandatory and permanent injunction and also for recovery of damages/mense profit. Appellant pleaded that she had filed false and frivolous cases against him and his wife and hence sought removal of the Defendant from the suit property. Appellant also pleaded that his wife was subjected to various threats and violence in the hands of the Defendant on several occasions. Respondent/ Defendant (wife of Appellant's son) contested the suit stating that house property was acquired through joint family funds and thus not his self-acquired property. She further claimed suit property to be a shared household as per Section 2(s) of the DV Act and thus she has right to stay/reside in the shared household. Appellant sought decree on the basis of admission made by Respondent in application under Section 12 of DV Act as she has herself in her pleadings admitted him to be the owner of the suit property. Trial Court decreed the suit. High Court in appeal vide impugned order remanded the matter to the Trial Court for fresh adjudication in accordance with the directions given therein. Hence, the present appeal.

Hon'ble Apex Court Held, while dismissing/ allowing the appeal:

Held, while dismissing the Appeals:

The definition of shared household in Section 2(s) is an exhaustive definition. The first part of definition begins with expression "means" which is undoubtedly an exhaustive definition and second part of definition, which begins with word "includes" is explanatory of what was meant by the definition.

The use of both the expressions "means and includes" in Section 2(s) of Act, 2005 clearly indicate the legislative intent that the definition is exhaustive and shall cover only those which fall within the purview of definition and no other.

Right to residence under Section 19 is not an indefeasible right of residence in shared household especially when the daughter-in-law is pitted against aged father-in-law and mother-in-law. The senior citizens in the evening of their life are also entitled to live peacefully not haunted by marital discord between their son and daughter-in-law. While granting relief both in application under Section 12 of Act, 2005 or in any civil proceedings, the Court has to balance the rights of both the parties. The directions issued by High court adequately balances the rights of both the parties.

The definition of shared household given in Section 2(s) cannot be read to mean that shared household can only be that household which is household of the joint family of which husband is a member or in which husband of the aggrieved person has a share. The judgment in S.R. Batra v. TarunaBatra has not correctly interpreted Section 2(s) of Act, 2005 and the judgment does not lay down a correct law.

In view of the ratio laid down by this Court in the above case, the claim of the Defendant that suit property is shared household and she has right to reside in the house ought to have been considered by the Trial Court and non-consideration of the claim/defence is nothing but defeating the right, which is protected by Act, 2005.

The power under Order XII Rule 6 is discretionary and cannot be claimed as a matter of right. In the facts of the present case, the Trial Court ought not to have given judgment under Order XII Rule 6 on the admission of the Defendant as contained in her application filed under Section 12 of the D.V. Act. Thus, there are more than one reason for not approving the course of action adopted by Trial Court in passing the judgment under Order XII Rule 6. Thus, High Court was correct that the judgment and decree of the

Trial Court given under Order XII Rule 6 is unsustainable.

For the purposes of determination of right of Defendant under Sections 17 and 19 read with Section 26 in the suit in question the Plaintiff can be treated as "Respondent", but for the grant of any relief to the Defendant or for successful resisting the suit of the Plaintiff necessary conditions for grant of relief as prescribed under the Act, 2005 has to be pleaded and proved by the Defendant, only then the relief can be granted by the Civil Court to the Defendant.

The expression "save in accordance with the procedure established by law", in Section 17(2) of the Act, 2005 contemplates the proceedings in court of competent jurisdiction. Thus, suit for mandatory and permanent injunction/eviction or possession by the owner of the property is maintainable before a Competent Court. In Sub-section (2) the injunction is "shall not be evicted or excluded from the shared household save in accordance with procedure established by law". Thus, the provision itself contemplates adopting of any procedure established by law by the Respondent for eviction or exclusion of the aggrieved person from the shared household. Thus, in appropriate case, the competent court can decide the claim in a properly instituted suit by the owner as to whether the women need to be excluded or evicted from the shared household. The High Court in the impugned judgment has also expressed opinion that suit filed by the Plaintiff cannot be held to be non-maintainable which is correct.

In case, the shared household of a woman is a tenanted/allotted/licensed accommodation where tenancy/allotment/license is in the name of husband, father-in-law or any other relative, the Act, 2005 does not operate against the landlord/lessor/licensor in initiating an appropriate proceedings for eviction of the tenant/allottee/licensee qua the shared household. However, in case the proceedings are due to any collusion between the two, the woman, who is living in the shared household has right to resist the proceedings on all grounds which the tenant/lessee/ licensee could have taken in the proceedings. The embargo under Section 17(2) of Act, 2005 of not to be evicted or excluded save in accordance with the procedure established by law operates only against the "Respondent", i.e., one who is Respondent within the meaning of Section 2(q) of Act, 2005.

Although husband of the Defendant was not a necessary party but in view of the pleadings in the written statement, the husband was a proper party.

The order passed under D.V. Act whether interim or final shall be relevant and have to be given weight as one of evidence in the civil suit but the evidentiary value of such evidence is limited. The findings arrived therein by the magistrate although not binding on the Civil Court but the order having passed under the Act, 2005, which is an special Act has to be given its due weight.

There is no embargo in referring to or relying on an admissible evidence, be of a civil court or criminal court both in civil or criminal proceedings.

Accordingly, (i) the pendency of proceedings under Act, 2005 or any order interim or final passed under D.V. Act under Section 19 regarding right of residence not an embargo for initiating or continuing any civil proceedings, which relate to the subject matter of order interim or final passed in proceedings under D.V. Act, 2005. (ii) The judgment or order of criminal court granting an interim or final relief under Section 19 of D.V. Act, 2005 are relevant within the meaning of Section 43 of the Evidence Act and can be referred to and looked into by the civil court. (iii) A civil court is to determine the issues in civil proceedings on the basis of evidence, which has been led by the parties before the civil court. (iv) In the facts of the present case, suit filed in civil court for mandatory and permanent injunction was fully maintainable and the issues raised by the Appellant as well as by the Defendant claiming a right Under Section 19 were to be addressed and decided on the basis of evidence, which is led by the parties in the suit.

High Court rightly set aside the decree of the Trial Court and remanded the matter for fresh adjudication. Appeal dismissed.

TWENTY

RUHI VS. ANEES AHMAD AND ORS., 2020

Hon'ble Judges/Coram:

L. Nageswara Rao and Hemant Gupta, JJ.

Relevant Sections:

CRIMINAL MATTERS - MATTERS FOR/AGAINST QUASHING OF CRIMINAL PROCEEDINGS

No. of pdf Pages of the Original Judgment: 3

Equivalent Citation:

2020(1)ACR1098, I(2020)DMC485SC, 2020(1)RCR(Criminal)644 MANU/SC/0145/2020

Case Notes:

Learned Counsel for the Appellant further submits that the Appellant has been living at Kabir Nagar, Delhi and in accordance with the judgment of this Court reported in Rupali Devi v. State of Uttar Pradesh (MANU/SC/0499/2019 : 2019 (2) R.C.R. (Criminal) 795 : 2019 (5) SCC 384), it is not necessary that a complaint should be filed only at the place of the matrimonial home. Even the Courts at the place where the wife resides after leaving the matrimonial home will have jurisdiction to entertain a complaint Under Section 498-A of the Indian Penal Code.

Facts:

The complaint preferred by the Appellant to the Senior Superintendent of Police, Ghaziabad on 22.5.2014 had been transferred to the Police Station, Welcome Colony, Delhi, FIR No. 645/2014 was registered by the Police

Station Welcome Colony, North East, Delhi Under Sections498A,406 and 34 Indian Penal Code and Under Section 4 of the Dowry Prohibition Act, 1961. The 1st Respondent approached the High Court by filing an application for quashing FIR No. 645/2014. The High Court refused to quash the FIR. However, the High Court was of the view that the place of occurrence as per the FIR was Meerut and the Appellant did not reside with Respondent No. 1 at Delhi. In that view, the High Court directed the transfer of the FIR from Police Station, Welcome Colony, Delhi to Police Station Lisadi Gate, Meerut, U.P. which was the place of matrimonial home of the Appellant and the Respondent No. 1.

Hon'ble Apex Court Held, while dismissing/ allowing the appeal:

The courts at the place where the wife takes shelter after leaving or driven away from the matrimonial home on account of acts of cruelty committed by the husband or his relatives, would, dependent on the factual situation, also have jurisdiction to entertain a complaint alleging commission of offences Under Section 498-A of the Indian Penal Code.

Having considered the submissions made on behalf of the parties, we are of the view that the charge sheet that has been filed at Meerut should be transmitted to a competent court in the Karkardooma Courts, Delhi. The District & Sessions Judge, East District, Karkardooma Courts, Delhi shall assign the case to the concerned Court.

In view of the aforesaid, the appeal is allowed. The charge sheet filed pursuant to FIR No. 645/2014, P.S. Lisadi Gate, Meerut, U.P. stands transferred to Karkardooma Courts, Delhi. The prosecution shall be conducted by the Delhi Police.

Pending application(s), if any, shall stand disposed of.

Videos & Tv Shows On Law & Exim

List of some important videos & TV shows on Law & EXIM by Adv. Jayprakash Somani on his YouTube Channel 'Jayprakash Somani EXIM & Legal'

Legal Videos: Hindi -English

1) SLP in Supreme Court / Special Leave Petitions in the Supreme Court of India

2) Transfer of Civil & Criminal Cases by the Supreme Court of India / Transfer of Matrimonial Cases

3) Appellate Jurisdiction of the Supreme Court of India

4) Jurisdictions of the Supreme Court of India

5) Public Interest Litigation in the Supreme Court of India / PIL in Supreme Court

6) Article 32 Writ Petitions in the Supreme Court of India

7) Bail Matters Top 10 Supreme Court Cases

8) FIR Quashing in High Court & Supreme Court

9) Bail & Anticipatory Bail Matters in Supreme Court

10) Insolvency & Bankruptcy Matters in the Supreme Court

11) Insolvency & Bankruptcy Code 2016 Part 1

12) Insolvency & Bankruptcy Code 2016 Part 2

13) Insolvency & Bankruptcy Code 2016 Part 3

14) Corporate Liquidation Process

15) Supreme Court Rules & Procedures Webinar of 2.5 hour on Zoom

16) RDDBFI Act, 1993 (Introduction)

17) The Indian Contact Act 1872

18) Negotiable Instruments Act (Introduction)

19) How to avoid matrimonial disputes& some more videos

20) SEBI Matters in the Supreme Court

21) Matrimonial Matters: Supreme Court's 20 Case Laws

22) Consumer Matters Supreme Court's 20 Case Laws

23) Service Matters Supreme Court's 20 Case Laws

24) How to Search Lawyer for Your Matter

25) Property Matters Supreme Court's 20 Case Laws

26) Bail Matters: Supreme Court's 20 Case Laws

27) Supreme Court / High Court Vacation Benches

28) 69000 Teacher's Recruitment Matters of UP Government in the Supreme Court

29) Contempt of Court Matters in the Supreme Court

30) Advocate Act's Matters in the Supreme Court

31) Business Law Matters in the Supreme Court

32) Banking Matters in the Supreme Court

33) Labour Law Matters in the Supreme Court

34) Arbitration Matters in the Supreme Court

35) Careers in Law -Zoom Webinar by Adv. Jayprakash Somani

36) Civil Matters in the Supreme Court

37) Consumer Protection Act | Consumer Matters in the Supreme Court

38) Corporate Matters in the Supreme Court

39) Criminal Matters in the Supreme Court

40) Role of Respondent in the Supreme Court of India

41) Motor Vehicle Accident Matters in Supreme Court with case laws

42) Article 131 Original Suits in Supreme Court

43) PIL in Supreme Court/ Public Interest Litigations in the Supreme Court of India'

44) CAB Citizenship Amendment Bill is not Unconstitutional

45) Supreme Court of India Cases & Process – Marathi

46) Legal Services Export / Export of Legal Services

47) Transfer of Matrimonial Cases by the Supreme Court of India

48) Public Interest Litigation PIL

49) The Specific Relief Act (Introduction)

50) Corporate Insolvency Resolution Process CIRP

51) ABMM's Career 5 - Careers in Law

52) Transfer of cases by Supreme Court

53) Writ Petitions in High Court & Supreme Court of India

54) Supreme Court Jurisdictions - Appeals, SLP, Writ Petitions, Transfer, Original, Review, Curative

55) LEGAL INDIA TV Show: Cases Handled in Supreme Court

56) Corporate Liquidation Process

57) Legal Services Export / Export of Legal Services

58) Corporate Laws

59) Election Matters- Supreme Court's 20 Case Laws

60) Companies Act, 2013

62) Competition Act, 2002

63) Banking Matters - Supreme Court's 20 Case Laws

64) Election Matters in the Supreme Court

65) Armed Forces Tribunal Matters in the Supreme Court

66) Compassionate Appointment Service matter

67) Foreign Exchange Management Act FEMA

68) Foreign Trade Policy 2021-26 Proposed

69) Customs Act 1962

70) Narcotic Drugs and Psychotropic Substances Act, 1985 NDPS Act

71) Foreign Trade Development & Regulation Act, 1992

72) How to Search Good Advocate in the Supreme Court of India

73) Sr. Adv Vikas Singh's Interview in Nani Palkhivala Wednesday Law Club

PPP

EXIM Videos: Hindi -English

1) Yes, I can do Import Export Business Easily! 36 points excellent video in Hindi

2) Yes, I can do Import Export Business Easily! 36 points excellent video in English

3) Import Export Business – Hindi video

4) Import Export Business - English video

5) Export Import Marathi TV Interview

6) Scope for Commerce Students in International Business- TV Show

7) Scope for Management Student in International Business- TV Show

8) Scope for Engineering Students in International Business – TV Show

9) Women in International Business- TV Show

10) How to do Import Export Business Successfully!'

11) Where one can get full information on Import Export Business?

12) What to do import & export?

13) Import Export Workshop/ Training/Course/ Diploma

14) How to Start Import Export Business & How to grow it. Live Webinar

15) Success Stories & Failure Stories in Import & Export Business

16) For MSME Scope in Export & Import...

17) Exports In Agri. & Food Products – English & some more videos

18) Exports to Dubai, Aabudhabii. e. UAE

19) Jewellery Exports from India

20) How to attend EXIM workshop to become excellent Exporter

21) Import Export Best Training Course – Online & Offline

22) Agri Product Export

23) Scope for Woman in International Business

24) Management Graduates Scope in International Business

25) Pharma Product's Export

26) Best Import Export Course | Practical Training | Aaronica Global Exim

27) Import Export Business for Commerce Graduates

28) How Do I Get Export Orders? Finding International Buyers

29) What Is APEDA In Import Export Business?

30) Which Is The Best Product To Export From India?

31) EXIM Remark by Manoj Kumar Faridabad

32) EXIM Remarks by Mahesh Telangana

33) What Licenses I Need To Start Import/ Export?

34) How Can I Increase My Import Export Business?

35) Which Is Best B2B Website For Import/Export Business?

36) Export Import Management with Global Marketing

37) How to Start Export Import Business | 51 Points Video

38) Scope for Commerce & Other Graduates in International Business

39) BE A SUCCESSFUL EXPORTER FOR OUR NATION - Marathi video

40) Export of Textile , Cotton, Agri., Food, & other products & services

41) Exports from MP, CG, MH, GJ & CA in Fresh Fruits & Vegetables

42) Exports in Agri. & Food Products- Hindi

43) Start your Online/E-Commerce Business

44) How to Start Export Import Business & Grow it

45) Exports in Textile & Other Products

46) Start and grow EXIM business - Live English Webinar

47)'Import Export Business!' Why, Who, What & How can one do it easily!!

48) Live: Export of Product & Services During & After Lock Down Period

49) Frauds in Import Export Business

50) Import Export for Business Man

51) Import & Export for Women

51) Import & Export for Graduate & Post - Graduate Students

52) Agriculture Exports from India

53) Digital Marketing Setup - Marathi

54) 2nd Secret of Successful Businessman

55) Digital Marketing Set up

56) Legal Services Export / Export of Legal Services

57) Export & Import with UAE

58) Service Exports / Exports by Service Providers

59) Import Export Workshop/ Training/Course/ Diploma

60) Exports & Imports with USA

61) Selection on Product for Export

62) Top Products Exported from India

63) What to do import & export?

64) ABMM Career 2 - 'Careers in Business & Industries

65) How to do Import Export Business Successfully!'

66) 5 Secrets of Successful Businessman

67) Export from MP, Chhattisgarh & Vidarbha Nagpur

68) EXIM Hindi - Textile & Apparel Export

69) EXIM Hindi - Export Import Practical Training In Delhi, Kolkata, Mumbai and Pune

70) Import Export Business

71) Import Export Business Hindi

72) Import Export Business English video

73) Import Export Business Marathi

74) Women in International Business by Exim Guru Adv. Jayprakash Somani

75) Opportunities in Foreign Trade- Adv. Jayprakash Somani's special interview

76) Textile Exports

77) India's Number in Exports. How to improve it?

78) 11 Benefits of Exim Workshop

79) Export Import Management with Global Marketing- 13 days Training Workshop

80) Cosmetic's Export

82) Export After COVID

83) Spices Exports

84) Handicraft Export

85) 10 Products India Exports to the World

List Of Adv. Jayprakash Somani's Books

1. Supreme Court of India's Leading Case Laws on 'Insolvency & Bankruptcy Code 2016'

2. Bail Matters – Supreme Court's Latest Leading Case Laws

3. Arbitration Matters- Supreme Court's Latest Leading Case Laws

4. Property Matters - Supreme Court's Latest Leading Case Laws

5. Matrimonial Matters- Supreme Court's Latest Leading Case Laws

6. Election Matters- Supreme Court's Latest Leading Case Laws

7.SEBI Matters- Supreme Court's Latest Leading Case Laws

8. Banking Matters- Supreme Court's Latest Leading Case Laws

9. Service Matters- Supreme Court's Latest Leading Case Laws

10. Contempt of Court Matters- Supreme Court's Latest Leading Case Laws

11. Consumer Protection Matters- Supreme Court's Latest Leading Case Laws

12. Corporate Law- Supreme Court's Latest Leading Case Laws

13. Supreme Court's AOR Exam- Leading Cases

14. Armed Force Tribunal - Supreme Court's Latest Leading Case Laws

15. Acquittal From 376 - Supreme Court's Latest Leading Case Laws

16. Negotiable instrument – Supreme Court's Latest Leading Case Laws

17. Contract Act- Supreme Court's Latest Leading Case Laws

18. Insider trading- Supreme Court's Latest Leading Case Laws

19. Foreign Exchange and Management Act- Supreme Court's Latest Leading Case Laws

20. Income Tax Act- Supreme Court's Latest Leading Case Laws

21. Company Law- Supreme Court's Latest Leading Case Laws

22. Competition & Monopoly Matters- Supreme Court's Latest Leading Case Laws

23. Compassionate Appointment- Service Matters- Supreme Court's Latest Leading Case Laws

24. Compulsory Retirement- Service Matters- Supreme Court's Latest Leading Case Laws

25. Voluntary Retirement- Service Matters- Supreme Court's Latest Leading Case Laws

26. Removal/Dismissal/Termination from Service- Supreme Court's Latest Leading Case Laws

27. Seniority- Service Matter- Supreme Court's Latest Leading Case Laws

28. Promotion- Service Matter- Supreme Court's Latest Leading Case Laws

29. Equal Pay for Equal Work- Service Matter- Supreme Court's Latest Leading Case Laws

30. Condition of Service- Service Matter- Supreme Court's Latest Leading Case Laws

31. Customs Act- Supreme Court's Leading Case Laws

32. Information Technology Act- Supreme Court's Latest Leading Case Laws

33. SEC. 125 CR. P. C.- Supreme Court's Latest Leading Case Laws

34. SEC. 498A OF I. P. C.- Supreme Court's Latest Leading Case Laws

⚐⚐⚐

These Books are available online at

1. **Notion Press:** https://notionpress.com/author/jayprakash_somani
2. **Amazon:** https://www.amazon.in/s?k=jayprakash+somani
3. **Flipkart:** https://www.flipkart.com/search?q=Jayprakash%20Somani

⚐⚐⚐

9 798886 674132

Printed by Libri Plureos GmbH in Hamburg, Germany